DK EYEWITNESS WORKBOOKS

Ancient Greece

by Kate Scarborough

Editorial Consultant Dr. Lindsay Allen
Educational Consultants Linda B. Gambrell and Geraldine Taylor

Senior Editors Rob Houston, Ankush Saikia, Fleur Star
Senior Art Editor Sarah Ponder
Editor Avanika
US Editor Megan Douglass
Art Editors Mahua Mandal, Tanisha Mandal
Assistant Editor Lisa Stock
DK Picture Library Claire Bowers, Romaine Werblow
Managing Editors Christine Stroyan, Shikha Kulkarni
Managing Art Editors Anna Hall, Govind Mittal
DTP Designers Dheeraj Arora, Anita Yadav
Production Editor Tom Morse
Production Controller Rachel Ng
Senior Jacket Designer Suhita Dharamjit
Jacket Design Development Manager Sophia MTT
Publisher Andrew Macintyre
Art Director Karen Self
Publishing Director Jonathan Metcalf

This American edition, 2020
First American edition, 2008 as
Published in the United States by DK Publishing
1450 Broadway, Suite 801, New York, NY 10018

20 21 22 23 24 10 9 8 7 6 5 4 3 2 1
001-323001-Jun/2020

A catalog record for this book is available from the Library of Congress.
ISBN: 978-0-7440-3449-3

Printed and bound in Canada

For the curious

www.dk.com

Contents

Fast Facts

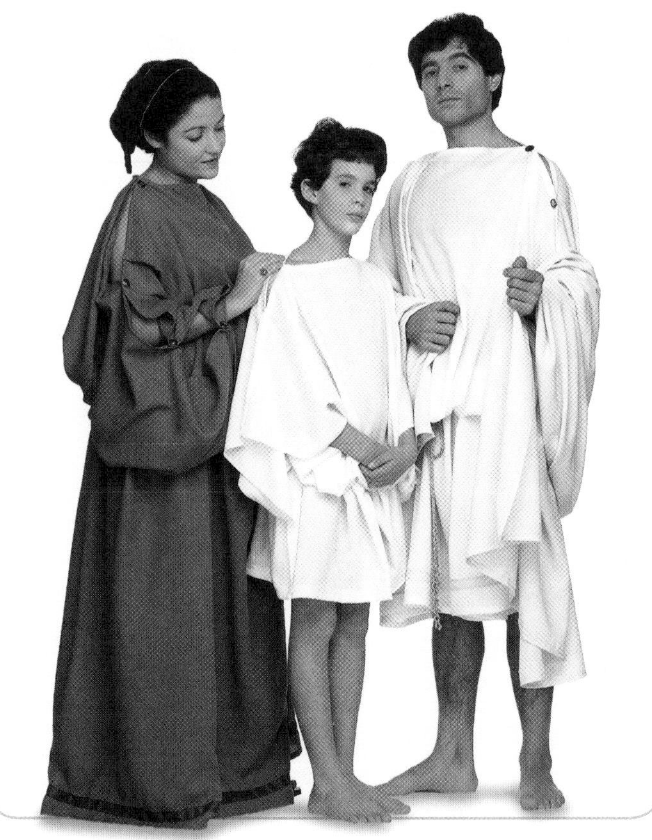

Activities

Quick Quiz

How This Book Can Help Your Child

Eyewitness Workbooks offer a fun and colorful range of stimulating titles on the subjects of history, science, and geography. Devised and written with the expert advice of educational consultants, each workbook aims to:

- develop a child's knowledge of a popular topic
- provide practice of key skills and reinforce classroom learning
- nurture a child's special interest in a subject

About this book

Eyewitness Workbook Ancient Greece is an activity-packed exploration of the lives and history of the ancient Greeks. Inside you will find:

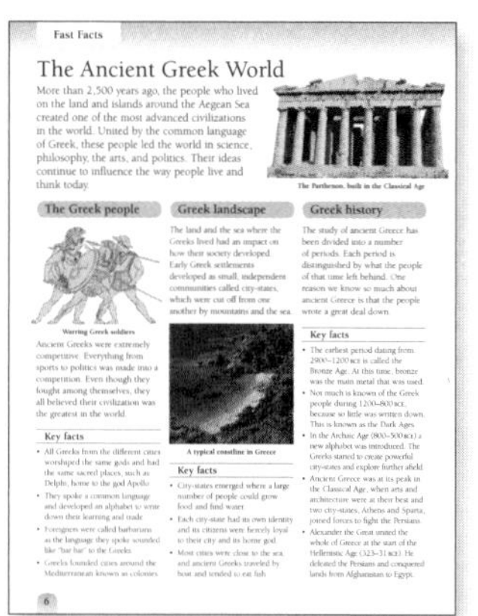

Fast Facts

This section presents key information as concise facts that are easy to digest, learn, and remember. Encourage your child to start by reading through the valuable information in the Fast Facts section and studying the statistics charts at the back of the book before trying out the activities.

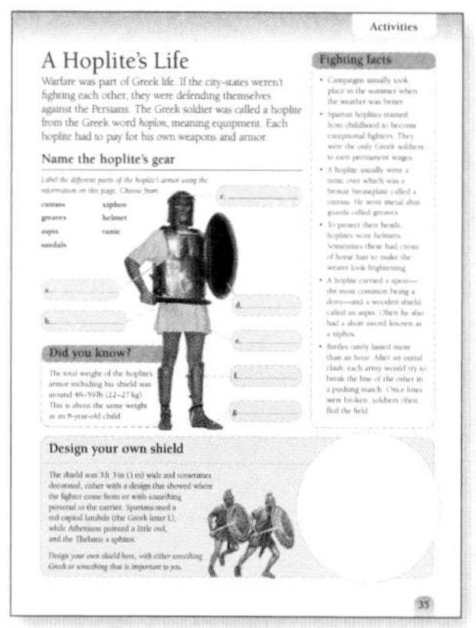

Activities

The enjoyable, fill-in activities are designed to develop information recall and help your child practice cross-referencing skills. Each activity can be completed using information provided on the page, in the Fast Facts section, or on the charts at the back of the book.

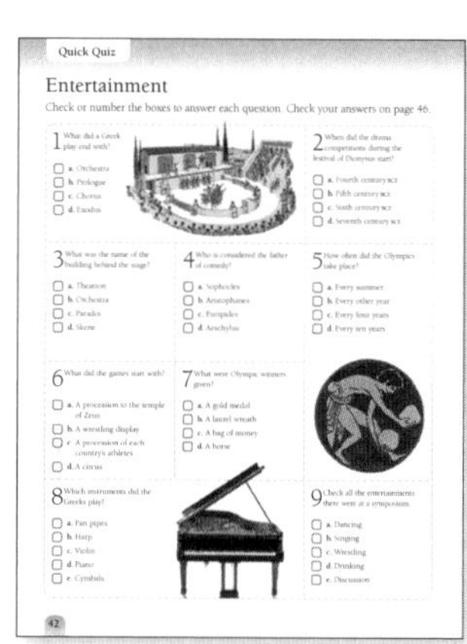

Quick Quiz

There are six pages of multiple-choice questions to test your child's newfound knowledge of the subject. Children should only try answering the quiz questions once all of the Activities section has been completed.

Important information

- The dates in this book are written as BCE ("Before Common Era") and CE ("in the Common Era"). BCE is comparable to BC, or "Before Christ," so 500 BCE is the same as 500 BC. CE is comparable to AD, or "Anno Domini," which is Latin for "year of the Lord," so 500 CE is the same as AD 500.
- Supervise your child when he or she is doing the cooking activity on page 29, and help them to thread the needle in the "Weave your own cloth" activity on page 25. Also make sure your child takes care using scissors in the "Make your own chiton" activity on page 31.

PROGRESS CHART

Chart your progress as you work through the activity and quiz pages in this book. First check your answers, then color in a star in the correct box below.

Page	Topic	Star	Page	Topic	Star	Page	Topic	Star
14	A World of City-States	☆	24	In the Home	☆	34	Olympic Games	☆
15	Knossos	☆	25	Women's Lives	☆	35	A Hoplite's Life	☆
16	Mycenae	☆	26	Buying and Selling	☆	36	Sea Battles	☆
17	Homer and the Trojan War	☆	27	A Greek Education	☆	37	Alexander the Great	☆
18	Athens	☆	28	Fun and Games	☆	38	History of Ancient Greece	☆
19	Politics and Power	☆	29	Wining and Dining	☆	39	Cities and Rulers	☆
20	Olympian gods and goddesses	☆	30	Greek Theater	☆	40	Greek Religion	☆
21	Heroes	☆	31	Clothing and Beauty	☆	41	Daily Life	☆
22	Sacred Sites	☆	32	The Scholars	☆	42	Entertainment	☆
23	Death and the Afterlife	☆	33	Science and Medicine	☆	43	Greeks at Work	☆

The Ancient Greek World

More than 2,500 years ago, the people who lived on the land and islands around the Aegean Sea created one of the most advanced civilizations in the world. United by the common language of Greek, these people led the world in science, philosophy, the arts, and politics. Their ideas continue to influence the way people live and think today.

The Parthenon, built in the Classical Age

The Greek people

Warring Greek soldiers

Ancient Greeks were extremely competitive. Everything from sports to politics was made into a competition. Even though they fought among themselves, they all believed their civilization was the greatest in the world.

Key facts

- All Greeks from the different cities worshiped the same gods and had the same sacred places, such as Delphi, home to the god Apollo.
- They spoke a common language and developed an alphabet to write down their learning and trade.
- Foreigners were called barbarians as the language they spoke sounded like "bar bar" to the Greeks.
- Greeks founded cities around the Mediterranean known as colonies.

Greek landscape

The land and the sea where the Greeks lived had an impact on how their society developed. Early Greek settlements developed as small, independent communities called city-states, which were cut off from one another by mountains and the sea.

A typical coastline in Greece

Key facts

- City-states emerged where a large number of people could grow food and find water.
- Each city-state had its own identity and its citizens were fiercely loyal to their city and its home god.
- Most cities were close to the sea, and ancient Greeks traveled by boat and tended to eat fish.

Greek history

The study of ancient Greece has been divided into a number of periods. Each period is distinguished by what the people of that time left behind. One reason we know so much about ancient Greece is that the people wrote a great deal down.

Key facts

- The earliest period dating from 2900–1200 BCE is called the Bronze Age. At this time, bronze was the main metal that was used.
- Not much is known of the Greek people during 1200–800 BCE, because so little was written down. This is known as the Dark Ages.
- In the Archaic Age (800–500 BCE) a new alphabet was introduced. The Greeks started to create powerful city-states and explore further afield.
- Ancient Greece was at its peak in the Classical Age, when arts and architecture were at their best and two city-states, Athens and Sparta, joined forces to fight the Persians.
- Alexander the Great united the whole of Greece at the start of the Hellenistic Age (323–31 BCE). He defeated the Persians and conquered lands from Afghanistan to Egypt.

Bronze Age Civilizations

Two impressive civilizations dominated the Greek world during the Bronze Age. On the island of Crete, south of mainland Greece, the vast palace at Knossos was discovered in the early 20th century. This was the center of the Minoan civilization. A more warlike society developed later on the mainland around the city of Mycenae.

The Minoans

Minoan culture developed on Crete from around 3000 BCE, reaching the height of their powers between 2000 and 1500 BCE. They had a big influence on early Greek life.

Key facts

- The civilization is called Minoan after the legendary King Minos who ruled at the city of Knossos.
- The Minoans traded with the Greeks, who copied their art and their writing system.
- The vast palace at Knossos was excavated by the English archaeologist Sir Arthur Evans. It had workshops, warehouses, and a sophisticated drainage system.
- By 1450 BCE, Knossos seems to have lost its power and Greeks took over the island of Crete.

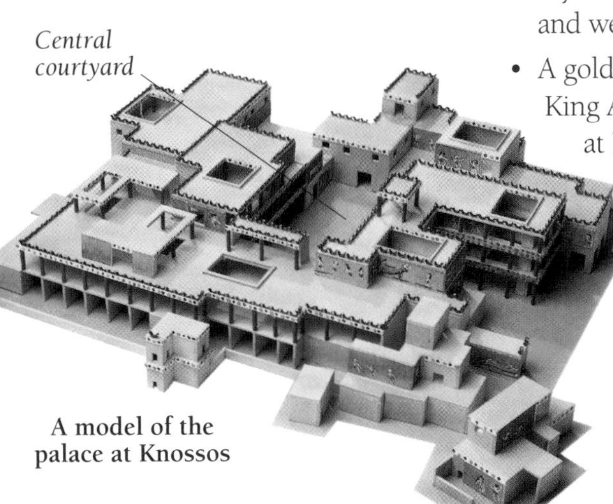

A model of the palace at Knossos

The Mycenaeans

During the Bronze Age, the Greeks on the mainland lived in small kingdoms centered on palaces, such as those at Mycenae, Pylos, Tiryns, and Thebes.

The so-called gold mask of Agamemnon

Key facts

- Mycenaean palaces were smaller than the palace at Knossos but were heavily fortified.
- Mycenaean kings were very wealthy and were buried with lots of gold.
- A gold mask named after legendary King Agamemnon was discovered at Mycenae in 1876 by the German archaeologist Heinrich Schliemann.
- The Mycenaeans' civilization reached its peak around 1600 BCE. By 1100 BCE its strongholds fell and the Dark Ages began.

Troy: fact or fiction?

The Greeks trick the Trojans with their wooden horse

Stories of the great Mycenaean civilization survived the Dark Ages and were told and retold from one generation to the next. Two stories in particular, the *Iliad* and the *Odyssey*, were made famous by the Greek poet Homer in his epic poems composed in the eighth century BCE. Homer told of the rivalry between the two cities of Mycenae and Troy. But how much of it is true?

Key facts

- In Homer's *Iliad*, Helen was the wife of Menelaus, king of Sparta, who was brother of Agamemnon, king of Mycenae. Helen was captured and taken to Troy by Paris, the son of Priam, king of Troy. This led to the Trojan war.
- Historians believe that it is possible the two cities fought, but over the ownership of land and crops rather than a woman.
- Homer's *Odyssey* is the story of the warrior Odysseus's return home to Ithaca after the Trojan war, with many adventures along the way.
- In 1870, German archaeologist Heinrich Schliemann discovered the site of ancient Troy—the city had been rebuilt nine times.

City-States

As Greece came out of the Dark Ages in the eighth century BCE, its cities grew in wealth and power. Each city was made up of the buildings and land around it. They operated as separate states with their own calendar, laws, public assemblies, and coins. One of the largest cities was Athens, which ruled over 1,000 sq miles (2,600 sq km).

Athens

The Acropolis, still standing in Athens today

Athens was the largest and richest city on mainland Greece. Its most striking and lasting achievement was the form of government it put in place after 510 BCE—democracy, or government by the people.

Key facts

- In 510 BCE the dictator Hippias was overthrown by Cleisthenes, a politician with new ideas.
- Every nine days, all male citizens could speak and vote on decisions taken in the ecclesia (assembly) held on the Pnyx hill.
- Cleisthenes replaced the four ruling families with ten new groups or tribes. Each tribe could select 50 members to a council that governed Athens on a day-to-day basis.
- In times of war, decisions were taken by 10 strategi, or generals, who were elected each year.

Sparta

Athens's biggest rival was Sparta, which had a very different culture. All the men were trained for war. They were ruled by two kings from two royal families and a council of 28 elders.

Key facts

- Spartan kings were generals in wartime, marching in front of their soldiers and performing sacrifices before battle.
- The powers of the kings were limited by five ephors who could arrest and depose them. The ephors were elected each year and oversaw the running of the state.
- Assemblies were held, but Spartan citizens could only agree to proposals or reject them by shouting instead of voting.

Leonidas, king of Sparta

Other cities

Greek cities, although ruled separately, were built along similar lines. The highest point of the city and the best defended was the acropolis. All cities also had an agora, or marketplace, for trade.

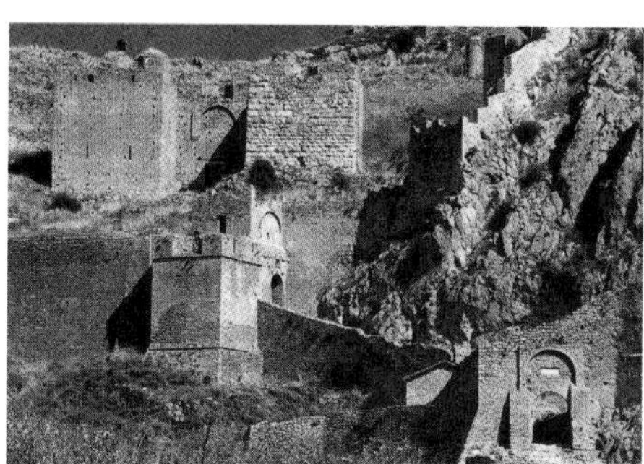

Corinth's strong fortifications were rebuilt several times over the centuries

Key facts

- Every city had its own emblem—Athens had an owl, Aegina had a turtle, and Corinth had a winged horse.
- Many cities created their own gymnasium, a place where the male citizens could train or exercise, and a theater, a place for entertainment.
- Some cities had a particular purpose in Greek life. Delphi was a city of oracles—a place where all Greeks could ask the god Apollo's priestess what life had in store for them.

Religion

The Greeks praised and feared many gods, who ruled over different areas of their lives. In order to lead a safe and happy life, people worshiped the gods who would, they believed, then take care of them. This worship took the form of building lavish temples, providing offerings, holding festivals, and making sacrifices. All of these helped keep the gods happy.

Temples

The columns of an ancient temple

Religion was extremely important in the life of the Greeks, so it is not surprising that their temples were their most impressive buildings. They also had political significance because they were used as a symbol of power and to celebrate success in war.

Key facts

- Temples were built with limestone or marble, with roofs and ceilings made of wood.
- Ox-drawn carts brought the large blocks of stone from quarries. Masons then carved them on site using chisels and hammers.
- The impressive columns were made from cylindrical drum sections, lifted into place with ropes and pulleys.
- Sculptors added decorative friezes around the top parts of the temple and in their triangular pediments.

Festivals

Every city had its own calendar of festivals to worship the gods. The ceremonies usually took place in the open air, inside a temenos (sanctuary). This was a special place away from ordinary life.

Key facts

- Religious festivals and ceremonies included processions, prayers, and sacrifices, and were held to ensure victory in war or a successful harvest.
- No one could enter a sanctuary if they were impure. Greeks believed people who had been in contact with death or childbirth were impure. They could be purified with water or with smoke from burning sulfur.

Athena's sanctuary at Delphi

Gods and goddesses

The most important gods belonged to one family led by Zeus, king of the gods. Zeus was responsible for the weather and is often seen with a thunderbolt in his hand. He was the father of many other gods.

Zeus, leader of the Greek gods

Key facts

- The Greeks believed that their gods lived on the highest mountain on the mainland, Mount Olympus.
- Each god represented a different part of life. Poseidon ruled the sea; Apollo, the sun; Hephaestus, fire; Aphrodite, love; Ares, war; and Artemis, hunting and the moon.
- Hades, brother of Zeus, was god of the underworld. He kidnapped the goddess Demeter's daughter, Persephone. Demeter was so upset that she stopped the crops from growing. Zeus persuaded his brother to let Persephone return to Earth for half the year, bringing spring and summer with her.
- Gods often had different names for different roles. Athena Polias was protector of Athens, while Athena Promachos (she who fights in front) was goddess of war.

Greeks at Home

The Greeks' lifestyle developed around the warm climate and their society. The houses they built were cool and dark, keeping out the heat. They ate the foods they found around them—fish from the sea and olives from the trees. They wore clothes that were simple to make and easy to clean and store.

Homes

Greeks built houses for protection and comfort. Outer windows were small, and living areas were not visible from the outside. Light came in through an open courtyard inside the outer walls.

Key Facts

- The walls of houses were built from mud bricks or rubble around a wooden frame. Sometimes the house had a stone base.
- The open courtyard in the center of the house connected all the rooms together. This courtyard was sometimes used as a garden for the house and held an altar.
- There was often an upper floor which was reached by a stepladder or stairs and was used for sleeping.
- The roofs of houses were covered with clay tiles, much like the tiles used in Greek villages today.

A modern Greek village with tile-roofed houses

Food

Ancient Greek food reflected their surroundings and was very simple as a result. People relied on wheat, olive oil, and wine. Sitting down at tables, they ate three meals a day prepared by the women of the household. Sometimes they used flat loaves of bread as plates, but more often they used clay bowls.

Key Facts

- Olives were pressed for olive oil, which was used in most Greek cooking. Grapes were picked for wine or left to dry in the sun to be eaten as sweet raisins.

Grapes were grown on sloping hillsides

- Most Greek towns were next to the coast so fishermen could catch fish and squid for the townsfolk to eat.
- Greeks rarely ate meat, but the more wealthy citizens could hunt for deer, boar, and hare. Most domestic animals, such as goats and hens, were kept for milk, cheese, and eggs rather than eaten.

Clothing

Typical dress of the ancient Greeks

Greek clothes were mostly spun from wool shorn from local sheep. The wool was spun very finely, so the clothes were much lighter than modern-day woolens. Sometimes flax was used to make linen. Rich Greeks also imported silk from the East.

Key Facts

- Greek clothes were not cut to fit. Their simple design made them easy to clean and store, and kept the wearer cool.
- Women wore a chiton, a single piece of cloth cut into two and fastened at intervals along the arms with pins.
- Men wore tunics, similar to the chiton but shorter, and carried a cloak called a himation.
- When indoors, the Greeks went around with bare feet, but outdoors they wore sandals with leather straps.

Greeks at Work

In ancient Greek cities, craftsmen worked in workshops surrounding the agora, or marketplace. People came to buy their products and farmers came into town to sell their produce in the agora. Most Greeks didn't travel far from home, but traders set sail, rather than cross mountains, to reach other city-states and countries.

Life at sea

The Aegean Sea offered plenty of food, and therefore work, to a large number of Greeks. The sea also allowed Greek traders to travel in ships to foreign lands taking with them Greek produce in exchange for other goods.

Key Facts

- The fishermen headed out with their nets and bronze hooks to catch local fish and seafood.
- They sold their catch both at the seaside and at the market.
- Traders lived dangerously—their boats were slow and often attacked by pirates. Thousands of ancient shipwrecks have been found in the Mediterranean!
- Early traders bartered (exchanged) goods. Trading became much simpler when coins were invented in the late sixth century BCE.

Fishing is still important to Greeks today

Farming

An olive grove

The land on the mainland of Greece and its islands is dry and rocky. Little grows easily apart from olive trees. Farming in Greece was hard, especially when growing barley and wheat for bread.

Key Facts

- The farmer's work ran in cycles. They plowed in the fall and spring with oxen, using wooden plows they made themselves.
- Farmers built flat terraces on hillsides to make growing olive trees and vines easier.
- Olives were used for food, oil, lighting, and cosmetics.
- The number of farm animals was limited by the size of the farm. Goats were the most common farm animal kept for their milk, cheese, and hair. They could climb rocky hillsides and ate anything, even thorny plants.

Crafts

The Greeks developed a wide range of crafts inspired by their need not just to survive but also to worship their gods. Architects and masons built their huge public buildings, while potters, sculptors, and bronze workers decorated them.

Key Facts

- The Greeks were famous for their beautiful pottery. Each city had its own potters' area where pots were made and sold.
- Craftsmen used enslaved people as helpers. Giving most of their profit to their slaveholders, the enslaved could save to buy their freedom.
- Sculptors learned their trade as apprentices to master sculptors.
- Bronze was useful to the Greeks, and old bronze statues were melted down and used again.

Atlas carrying the world on his shoulders

A marble sculpture of the god Atlas

Entertainment

The ancient Greeks worked hard, but they also had plenty of time to enjoy themselves. Some of their entertainments, such as the theater, were also held to give pleasure to the gods. Other events, such as the Olympic games, reflected their competitive nature and their desire to demonstrate their strength.

Fun and games

Wealthy Greeks, especially those living in cities, had plenty of time for fun. Music was particularly important. Evidence of games has survived mainly in sculpture, paintings, and writings.

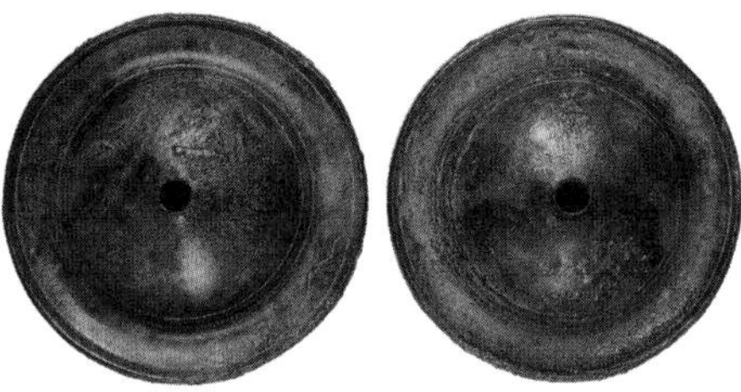

Bronze cymbals

Key Facts

- Greeks sang at births, weddings, and funerals. They wrote love songs, battle songs, and songs of thanksgiving to the gods to celebrate the harvest.
- Greek instruments were similar to the ones we use today. They had stringed instruments, such as the harp and the lyre, as well as wind instruments, such as pan pipes.
- Along with music came dancing. It seems from wall paintings that Greek women danced for their men at celebrations and drinking parties.
- Some vases show warriors playing board games, and gaming pieces made from bone, clay, and stone have been found.

Olympics

The Greeks valued sports as training for warfare and as a way of honoring the gods. There were many local sporting competitions, but the biggest was the Olympic games, held every four years at Olympia.

Key Facts

- Wars were suspended during the Olympics to allow people to travel to the games safely.
- Success in the games brought honor to the athlete's family and to his home town. Some victors were given almost mythical status.
- Discipline in sports was strict. Breaking the rules was severely punished.

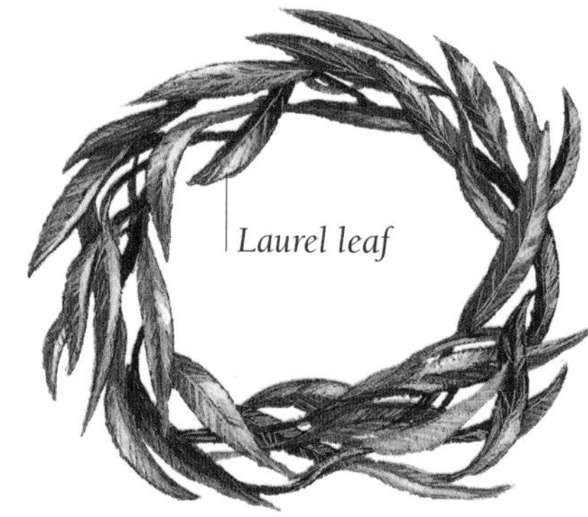

Victors were crowned with a laurel wreath

- The games went on into Roman times, coming to an end in the late fourth century CE.

Theater

Greek theaters are among the most spectacular buildings that survive from ancient times. They have huge semicircles of tiered seating around a central stage. Some theaters could hold over 15,000 people.

The ruins of a Greek theater

Key Facts

- From the middle of the sixth century BCE, drama competitions took place during the spring festival of the Dionysia.
- By the fifth century BCE, both tragedies and comedies were performed.
- The actors were all men and they wore masks on stage. Only three could ever talk to one another on the stage in one scene.
- A larger group of actors, called the chorus, commented on the action of the play.
- Music accompanied the plays, which were acted out on a flat area called the orchestra.

A masked actor

The Hellenistic Age

In the fourth century BCE, a strong king called Philip II turned Macedonia into the most powerful state in Greece. After he was assassinated in 336 BCE, his 20-year-old son, Alexander, took over. Alexander conquered the whole of Greece and went on to take his army into Asia Minor, Afghanistan, India, and Egypt.

Spread of traditions

After Alexander's death his generals fought among themselves and eventually divided his empire into kingdoms which they ruled themselves. The influence of ancient Greece lasted from 323 BCE to 30 BCE.

Philip of Macedonia

King Philip II was a good general. He formed a Macedonian army which conquered Thrace and Thessaly. He was in the process of uniting all the Greek cities against the Persians when he was assassinated.

Key Facts

- Philip ruled the Macedonians who were looked down on by many Greeks (especially Athenians) as being almost barbarian.
- Philip married several times and had many children. The wife he called Olympias gave birth to Alexander.
- Philip appointed the philosopher Aristotle as Alexander's tutor.
- Aristotle taught Alexander rhetoric (the art of persuasive speaking), literature, science, medicine, and philosophy.

Aristotle

Alexander the Great

A young Alexander taking control of his soldiers

Alexander was one of the wonders of the ancient world. He was a military genius, leading over 35,000 soldiers into Asia to conquer the Persian Empire.

Key Facts

- Alexander's first great achievement was to tame the wild horse Bucephalus when he was just 12.
- Alexander's greatest enemy was Darius III of Persia. He fought two battles against him to defeat him and crown himself king of Persia.
- Between 336 and 323 BCE, Alexander led his army as far as India and Egypt. He founded many new towns, and called them all Alexandria after himself.
- Alexander died in 323 BCE at the age of just 32.

Key Facts

- There were three large Hellenistic kingdoms: the Ptolemaic empire of Egypt, the Seleucid empire of Asia, and Macedonia.
- These states were bitter rivals and fought among each other for further power.
- During this time, Greek became an international language. Jewish writers chose to write the life of Jesus in Greek rather than in their native Hebrew.
- New cities were built around the empire in the Greek way, with temples, agoras, theaters, and gymnasiums.
- The Hellenistic Age ended with the expansion of the Roman empire.
- Pergamon, a Hellenistic city in Asia Minor, was the power base of one of the ruling generals. Its ruins show how beautiful the city was in ancient times.

The ruins of the Hellenistic city of Pergamon in Asia Minor (Turkey)

A World of City-States

During the Classical Age, Greece was divided into hundreds of cities, or poleis. Each one was ruled separately and developed its own form of society. Sometimes the poleis formed alliances against the common enemy, the Persians. More often they fought each other for land and supremacy.

Did you know?

A Classical Greek city usually had a high, fortified area called an acropolis, meaning "high city." This was often where the most important temples were built.

Where's where?

Add the missing city names to the dots. Use the map on page 8 to help you.

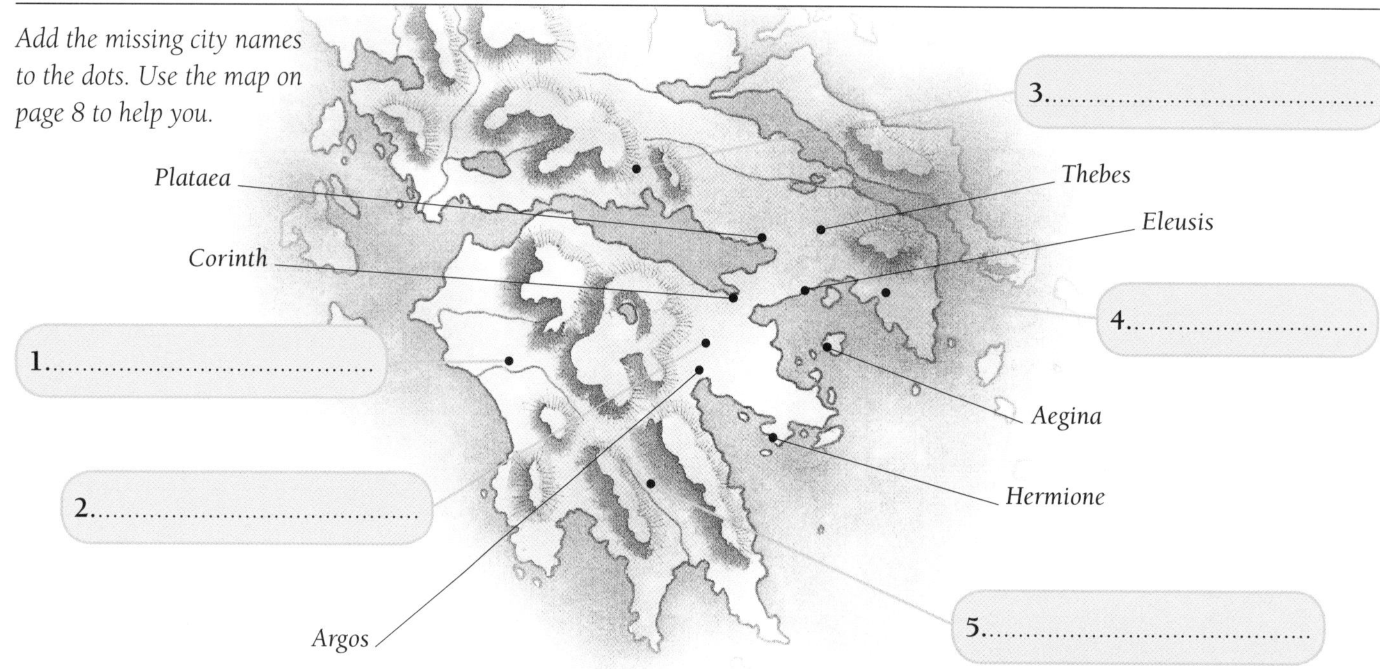

Fill in the dates

Historians divide ancient Greek development into periods, or ages. Choosing from the dates below, and using the information on page 6, fill in the missing dates.

2900–1200 BCE **323–30** BCE **800–500** BCE **1200–800** BCE **500–323** BCE

Lion's Gate in Mycenae

Bronze Age ....

Pottery

Dark Age ....

Kouros statue

Archaic Age ....

Delphi column

Classical Age ....

Hellenistic coin

Hellenistic Age ....

Knossos

When Sir Arthur Evans started to work on the site of Knossos, he quickly realized that it was one of the most important ceremonial and political centers of the Bronze Age. The great palace at Knossos was built between 1700 and 1400 BCE and is thought to be the inspiration behind the legend of Theseus and the Minotaur.

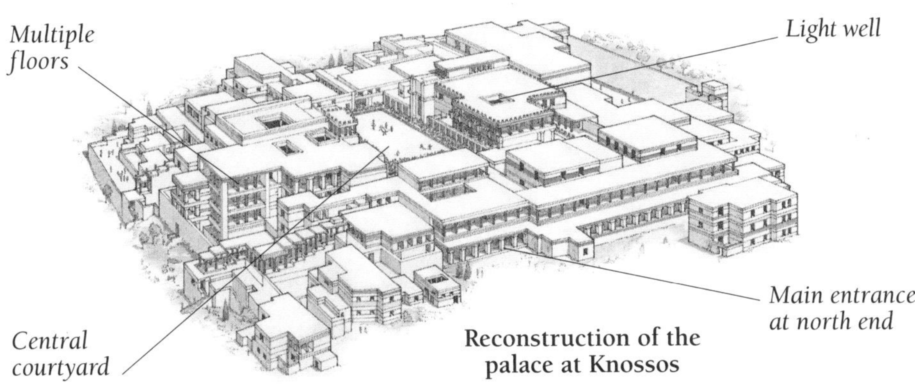

Reconstruction of the palace at Knossos

Theseus and the Minotaur

Coin from Knossos with a labyrinth design

Read this story and page 7 to fill in the answers below.

King Minos had beaten the Athenians in battle and demanded that every nine years, seven Athenian boys and seven Athenian girls be sent to him to be fed to the minotaur—a hideous creature, half-man and half-bull, kept in the depths of a labyrinth (maze).

On the third occasion, the king's son Theseus went with the group to kill the Minotaur and save his people. He tricked Ariadne, Minos's daughter, into falling in love with him. She gave him a sword and ball of wool so he could find his way out of the maze. Theseus killed the Minotaur, rescued his people, and escaped with Ariadne. On his return home, he abandoned Ariadne on the island of Naxos.

1. On which island was Knossos?

....

2. How many Athenians in total were sent to their deaths on Crete?

....

3. What was the minotaur?

....

4. Who was the king's daughter?

....

5. What did she give Theseus to help him?

....

6. Where was she abandoned?

....

Make a maze

Using a checkered board, some string, and putty, try making your own maze.

1 Use string to create a route over the checker board. Try to cover as much of the board as possible. Make a clear entrance and exit.

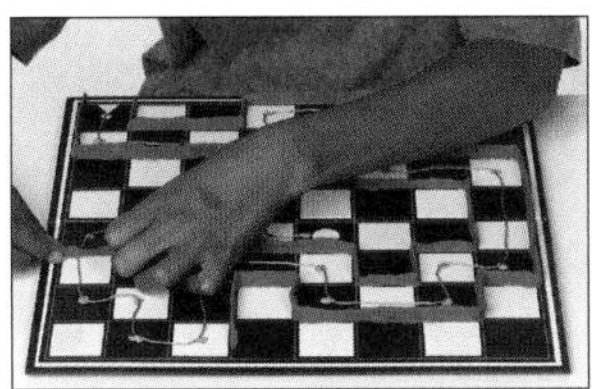

2 Build walls along your route with putty.

3 Create false walls and trick routes to make your route hard to find.

4 Take away the string that highlights your route.

5 Use a ball to see if a friend can work his or her way around your maze.

Mycenae

In legends, Mycenae was the city of King Agamemnon. Remains show it was heavily fortified. The royal palace contained not just ceremonial rooms, but also the military headquarters and administrative buildings. The Mycenaeans were warriors as well as great traders.

Label the different parts of Mycenae

Label the different parts of Mycenae, using the descriptions below.

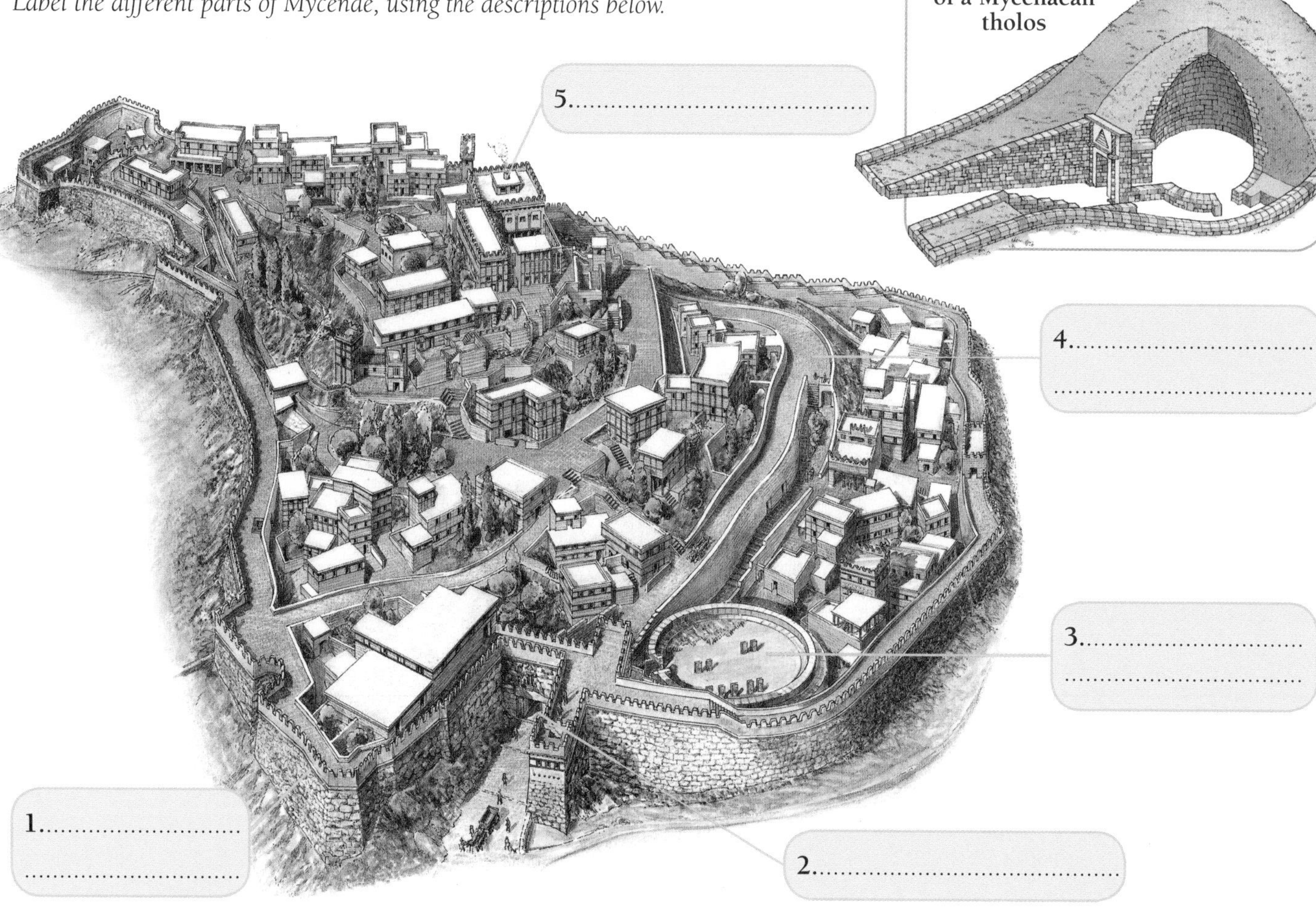

A rich burial

Some rich Mycenaean kings and warriors were buried in dome-shaped structures like this one, called a tholos. With their bodies, archaeologists have also found weapons, armor, and jewelery made from gold, bronze, and boar tusks.

Cross-section of a Mycenaean tholos

A view of Mycenae

- The main entrance to the city, known as the **Lion's Gate**, was tucked into the fortified walls.
- The **King's palace** sat on the highest point of the city with views of the countryside.
- The **Grave circle** was where the famous Agamemnon's mask was found along with many other golden artifacts.
- The **walls of the city** were over 16 feet (5 m) thick in places and surrounded the whole city.
- The **Great Ramp** led from the Lion's Gate up to the king's palace.

Did you know?

No one knows if Agamemnon was a real person or a myth. He is said to have married Clytemnestra and had four children. He gathered an army to attack Troy, but angered the gods and met with bad luck. After the war, he returned to Greece but was murdered by his wife.

Homer and the Trojan War

Storytellers called rhapsodists went from town to village entertaining people with their stories. Whether the stories were true or not was lost over time. The most famous of these stories, the *Iliad* and the *Odyssey*, were finally written down, supposedly by the poet Homer.

Who's on which side?

Fill in the names of the Greek and Trojan heroes and heroines fighting over Helen in the facts on this page.

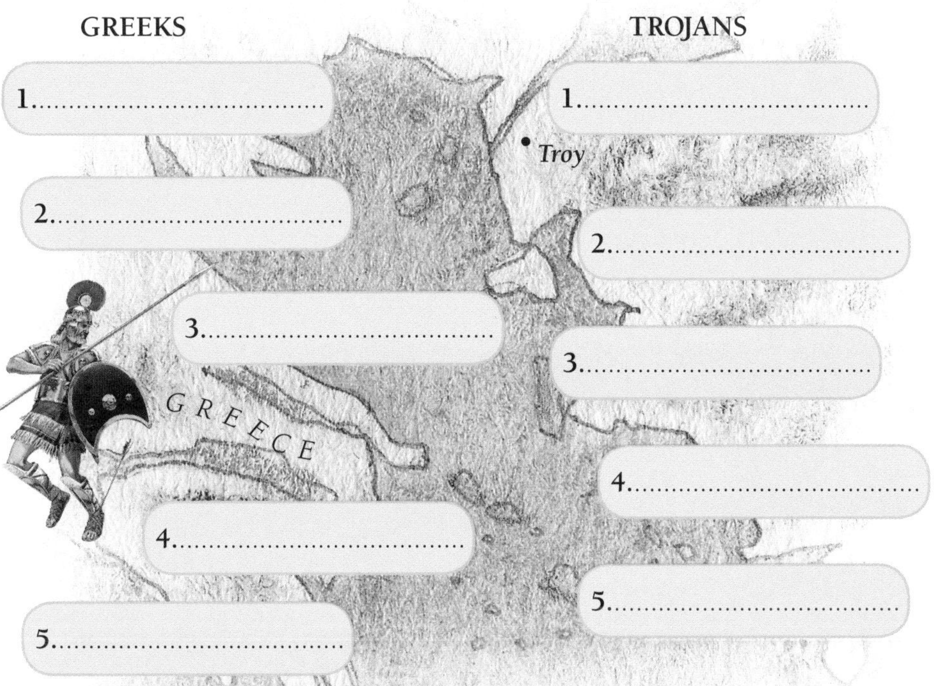

Trojan War heroes

- **Paris**, prince of Troy, fell in love with Helen, wife of **Menelaus**, the king of Sparta, and took her away.
- Menelaus's brother, **Agamemnon,** helped form an army to attack Troy.
- Agamemnon and his fiercest warrior, **Achilles,** argued, and Achilles left the battle.
- Achilles' best friend **Patroclus** pretended to be Achilles and led an attack. He was killed by **Hector**, son of **Priam** the king of Troy.
- **Cassandra**, Priam's daughter, foresaw the fall of Troy but was struck dumb by Apollo.
- Achilles was so enraged by Patroclus's death that he joined the battle and killed Hector.
- One of the surviving Greek warriors, **Odysseus**, was the hero of Homer's epic *Odyssey*.
- **Aeneas**, Troy's only surviving warrior, founded Rome according to the Roman poet Virgil in his epic, the *Aeneid*.

Odysseus and Polyphemus quiz

Circle the correct word to finish these sentences and make sense of this story from the Odyssey.

1. Odysseus and his men were imprisoned by a giant shepherd called **Paris / Polyphemus / Hector.**
2. Polyphemus had just one central eye. He was a **gorgon / Cyclops / griffin.**
3. Odysseus tricked Polyphemus into drinking too much **milk / wine / oil.**
4. As Polyphemus lay drunk on the ground, Odysseus took a hot wooden stake and pierced his **ear / eye / toe.**
5. Blinded, Polyphemus couldn't see Odysseus and his men escaping under the bellies of his **rabbits / sheep / frogs.**

Odysseus blinding the cyclops Polyphemus

Athens

The strongest of all the Greek city-states, Athens has a colorful history. It was the birthplace of democracy and also a great and powerful defender of the Greek lands. Within Greece, Sparta was its most ferocious enemy, but abroad, the massive Persian empire was a constant threat.

The Parthenon

After the Persian defeat in 479 BCE Athens's Acropolis was rebuilt by Pericles. The Parthenon was the main temple, dedicated to Athena.

Draw lines from the captions to the correct parts of the Parthenon.

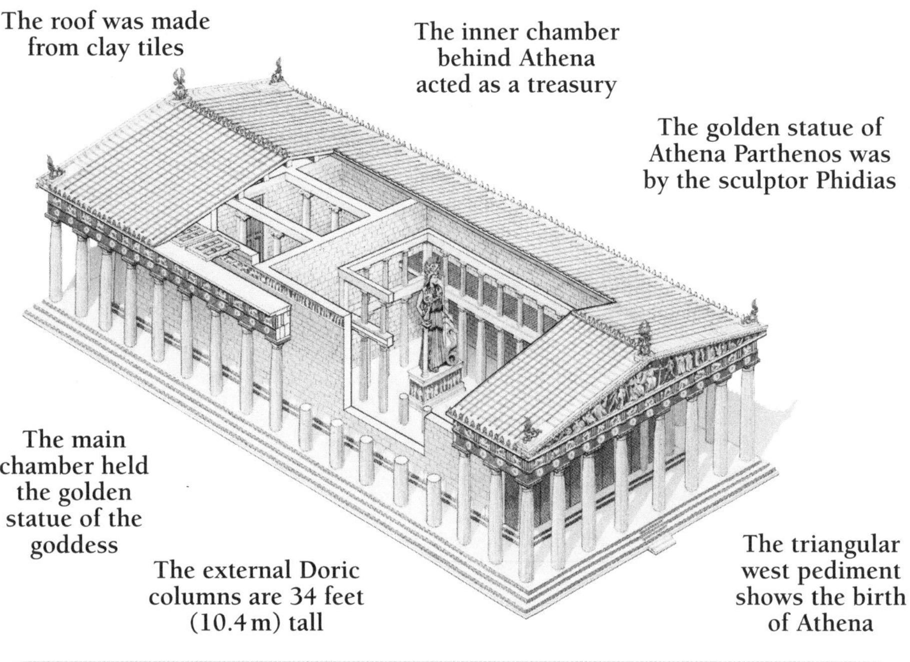
The roof was made from clay tiles
The inner chamber behind Athena acted as a treasury
The golden statue of Athena Parthenos was by the sculptor Phidias
The main chamber held the golden statue of the goddess
The external Doric columns are 34 feet (10.4 m) tall
The triangular west pediment shows the birth of Athena

Fill in the dates

Read through the Persian War facts to add the correct date—watch out, as the events listed below are not necessarily in the right chronological order!

1..........................
Battle of Plataea

2..........................
Battle of Marathon

3..........................
Xerxes' arrival in Greece

4..........................
Greek rebellion in Asia Minor

5..........................
Battle of Salamis

6..........................
Battle of Thermopylae

Persian soldiers

Persian War facts

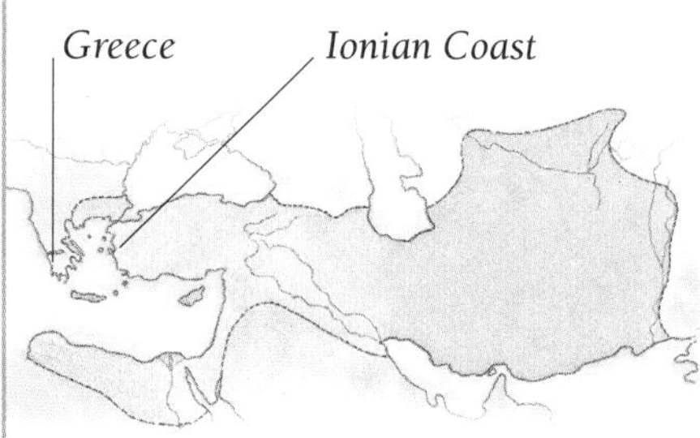
Greece
Ionian Coast

The Persian Empire (in green) in 490 BCE

- After **550 BCE**, many Greeks on the Ionian Coast of modern Turkey became part of the huge Persian empire.
- In **499 BCE**, some of these Greeks rebelled and were helped by the Athenians. The Persians crushed the rebellion.
- In revenge for Athens's involvement, in **490 BCE** the Persians crossed the Aegean Sea and landed troops on the plains of Marathon near Athens.
- The Athenians led by General Miltiades defeated the Persian force.
- In **480 BCE**, King Xerxes of Persia brought a massive force and defeated the Spartan-led army at Thermopylae.
- The Athenians took to their ships and defeated the Persian fleet at Salamis in **480 BCE**, as King Xerxes watched helplessly from a hilltop.
- Xerxes rushed back to Persia leaving behind a military force.
- A final battle between the Persians and Greeks took place at Plataea in **479 BCE**. The Greeks were victorious and the Persian threat to Greece was lessened.

Politics and Power

The Athenians developed a system of government that has become the inspiration for all democratic governments today—with one big difference. In Athens, only free men had a part to play in governing the city, while today all men and women have a say.

The Pnyx, where Athenians gathered for their Assembly

Democracy quiz

Use the information on this page to answer the following questions.

1 How many men sat on the council?

....

2 How large were the juries?

....

3 How many strategi were there?

....

4 How many votes were needed to ostracize someone?

....

5 How often were Assemblies held?

....

Did you know?

The philosopher Socrates was sentenced to death for being a bad influence on young Athenian men. He could have escaped, but out of respect for the Athenian system he drank poison from the hemlock plant.

Hemlock seeds

Democracy facts

- Every nine days an assembly was held at the Pnyx. All male citizens could speak and vote.
- Ten generals, called strategi, were elected each year to lead the Athenian army.
- Proposals for the Assembly came from the council, made up of 500 men drawn by lot from all citizens each year.
- There were no lawyers in Athens. Any citizen could bring a fellow citizen to trial. To prevent bribery, juries were large, from 101 to 1,001 men.
- If a citizen was found guilty of a crime, there were a number of punishments. To be exiled, or ostracized, a minimum of 6,000 men needed to vote against the person.

Famous Athenians

Match the person with their deeds. Use the chart at the back of the book and page 18 to help you.

a. **Miltiades**	1. masterminded the rebuilding of the Acropolis.
b. **Pericles**	2. led the fleet at the Battle of Salamis and defeated the Persians.
c. **Themistocles**	3. was a pupil of Socrates, writing down all his famous dialogs.
d. **Plato**	4. led the Athenian allies at Marathon.
e. **Thucydides**	5. wrote a history of the wars between Athens and Sparta.

Pericles

Olympian Gods and Goddesses

Greek gods and goddesses were immortal and had supernatural powers but they were also very human. They fought each other, and could be jealous and angry.

Greek gods' family tree

Using the information on this page, fill in the missing names in this divine family tree.

Kronos + 1...............

Hestia

Demeter + Zeus

Leto + Zeus + Metis

3.................. + Hades

2.......................

4.............. + Zeus

6........................

5.................. Artemis Ares Hebe Hephaestus

Did you know?

Athena, the goddess of Athens, was the daughter of Zeus. It was said that she was born from Zeus's head. She was linked to warfare and wisdom and is often seen holding an owl. The owl, because of its unblinking eyes, was considered wise.

Divine offspring

- Kronos's wife was Rhea. They had six children: Zeus, Hestia, Hera, Demeter, Hades, and Poseidon.
- Zeus was husband to Hera and together they had Hephaestus, Hebe, and Ares.
- Zeus also fathered children with other goddesses. He and Demeter had Persephone, while Apollo's and Artemis's mother was Leto. Athena was Zeus's daughter by Metis.

Match the gods with nature

Every god or goddess had power over some part of nature. Use the information on pages 9 and 22 to help you match the god with the natural force. Choose from the gods below, then draw pictures to fill in the missing images.

Zeus Apollo Poseidon Artemis Hephaestus

1. Moon ....
2. Sea ....
3. Sun ....
4. Fire ....
5. Storm ....

Heroes

The gods and goddesses not only ruled over the lives of ordinary people, they even had children with them. Zeus was the father of the greatest Greek hero of them all, Hercules.

The twelve labors of Hercules

The goddess Hera hated Hercules because he was the son of Zeus and a mortal woman. She wanted to make life difficult for him, so she made him go mad, and in his madness he killed his wife and children. When he came out of his madness he was devastated and asked the god Apollo what he could do to regain his honor. Apollo told Hercules to work for his arch-enemy Eurystheus for twelve years. Eurystheus gave Hercules twelve seemingly impossible tasks. These he did and became forever the perfect Greek hero.

1. To kill the Nemean Lion.
2. To destroy the Lernaean Hydra.
3. To capture the Ceryneian Hind.
4. To trap the Erymanthian Boar.
5. To clean the Augean Stables.
6. To kill the Stymphalian Birds.
7. To capture the Cretan Bull.
8. To round up the Mares of Diomedes.
9. To steal the Girdle of Hippolyte.
10. To herd the Cattle of Geryon.
11. To fetch the Apples of the Hesperides.
12. To capture Cerberus, the guardian of Hades.

b.

Number these images to match the correct task. Use the information above to help.

c.

a.

Perseus and Medusa the Gorgon

Another of Zeus's children was Perseus. He was asked by Polydectes, the king of Seriphos, to bring him the head of Medusa. Medusa was a gorgon whose gaze turned people to stone. Perseus was helped by Athena, who gave him a highly polished shield, and Hermes, who gave him a curved sword. When he reached Medusa's cave, he approached the gorgon by looking at her reflection in the shield. Using the sword he cut off her head and wrapped it in a bag.

Use the information above to answer the following questions.

1. Who gave Perseus the task?

....

2. What was the name of the gorgon?

....

3. What did Athena give to Perseus to help him?

....

....

4. Who else helped Perseus?

....

5. Where did Perseus put the gorgon's head?

....

Perseus holding Medusa's head

Sacred sites

The Greeks celebrated their religious ceremonies on a sacred ground, called a temenos. These sites were built away from places of everyday living. The Greeks first built altars to help them offer prayers and sacrifice. Later, they built temples.

Temple of Artemis at Ephesus

Temples became more elaborate over the years. Each revealed the success and stature of the city that built it. Every city had its own calendar of festivals that were celebrated in and around the temple.

This is a cutaway of the temple of Artemis at Ephesus, named as one of the seven wonders of the ancient world. Read the descriptions below, then number the labels.

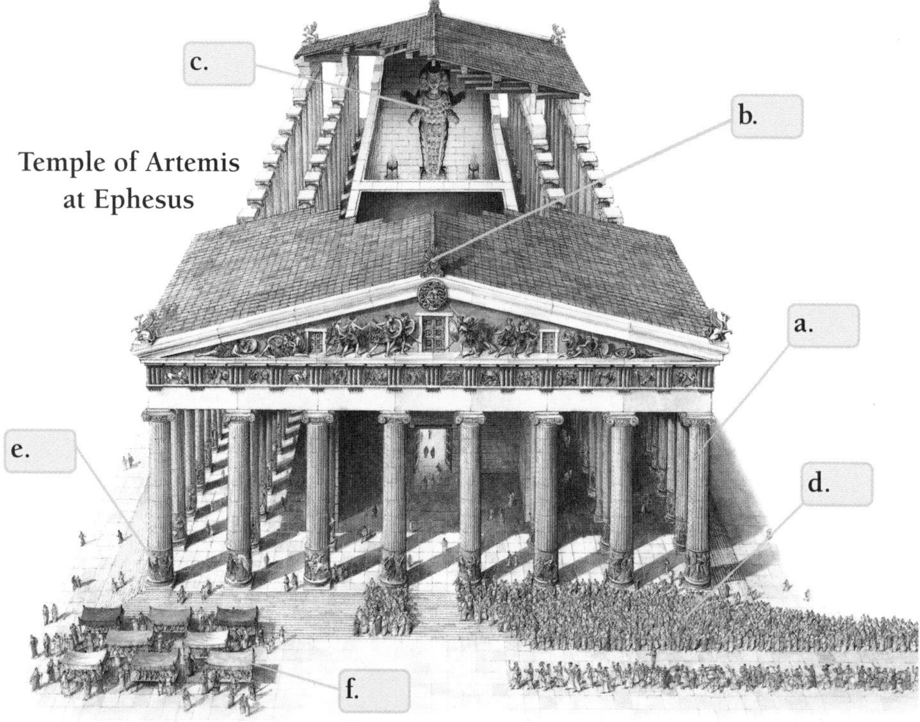

Temple of Artemis facts

1. A great procession heads to the temple to worship Artemis.
2. Stallholders sell miniature statues of Artemis.
3. The Ionic columns stand 60 ft (18 m) tall.
4. The bottoms of the columns were sculpted with figures in relief.
5. A marble Acroterion sculpture sits on top of the triangular pediment.
6. The great statue of Artemis stands inside the temple. She was not just the goddess of hunting and the moon, but also of fertility.

Spot the column

There are three different designs of column. Read the descriptions and find the right match for each one.

1. The **Doric** style is sturdy, and its top (the capital) is plain. It was used in mainland Greece and the colonies in southern Italy.

2. The **Ionic** style is thinner and more elegant than the Doric, with a scroll-like design on its capital. It was found in eastern Greece.

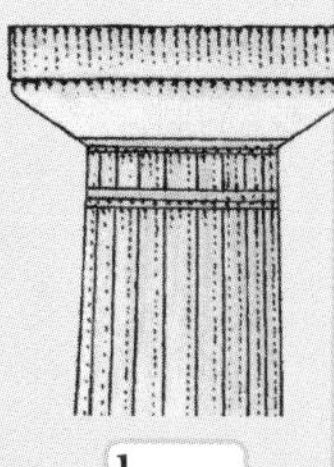

3. The **Corinthian** style was rare in Greece, but was popular on Roman temples. It has an elaborate capital with acanthus leaves.

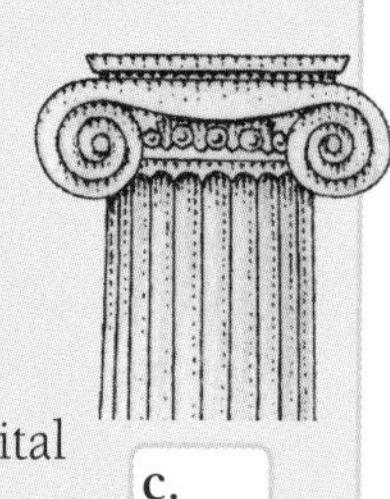

Did you know?

Greek altars could either be simple flat stones or much more elaborate constructions. Those in danger, such as runaway enslaved people, could throw themselves on the mercy of the gods at the altar. Killing anyone here would bring the gods' anger on the whole city.

Death and the Afterlife

Greeks had various ideas about death and the afterlife. Some thought that the ghosts of the dead lived in a miserable underworld named after its god, Hades. Funeral rites were very elaborate. This was partly to ensure that the dead person's soul did not come back to haunt the living.

Did you know?

It was thought that Hermes the messenger god took the dead person to the underworld. He handed them to an old boatman called Charon who ferried them across the river Styx to the kingdom of Hades. The dead had to pay Charon a small fee to cross the river, so a coin was placed in the mouth of the dead during funeral preparations.

Funeral rites

Number the statements below to create a proper Greek funeral.

Bronze dagger sheath

a. The body was cremated or buried. The body or its ashes were buried with some possessions.

Flask of oil

b. Once buried, the dead person was given offerings of water, honey, oil, and wine.

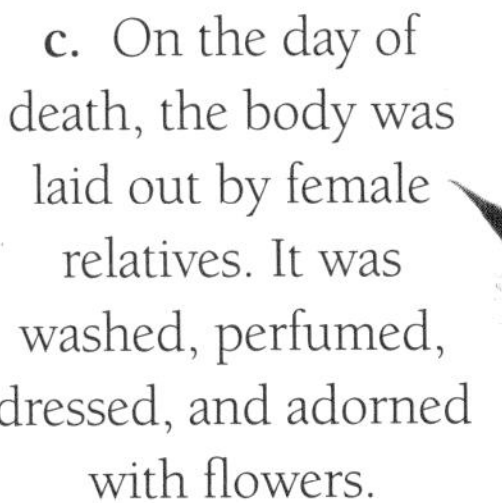

c. On the day of death, the body was laid out by female relatives. It was washed, perfumed, dressed, and adorned with flowers.

Myrtle

d. The Greeks believed that anyone in contact with a dead body needed purification. After the funeral the mourners washed with spring water. The house was also purified with water and sprigs of hyssop.

Hyssop sprig

e. Those who could afford it set up a memorial on the site of the loved one's tomb. This was a small carved stone slab called a stele. A stele could show a touching scene of the dead saying goodbye.

Gravestone

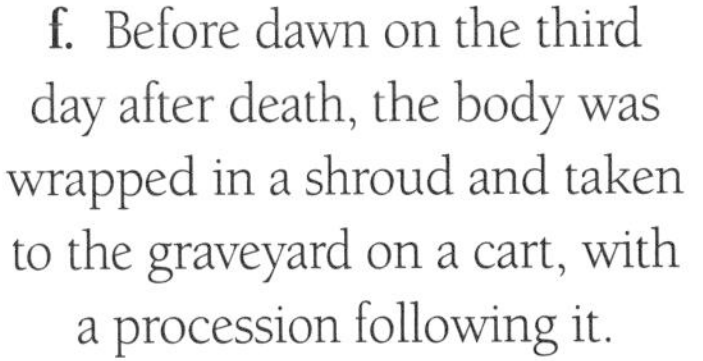

f. Before dawn on the third day after death, the body was wrapped in a shroud and taken to the graveyard on a cart, with a procession following it.

Hades and Persephone

Complete the following sentences to complete the story of Hades and Persephone. Use the information on page 9 to help you.

1. Hades was god of the ....
2. His brother was ....
3. Persephone's mother was ....
4. She stopped the growth of ....
5. Persephone was released from Hades for the seasons .... and ....

Hades kidnapping Persephone

In the Home

The Greeks liked their homes to be private. The walls were made from sun-dried mud bricks, which have not survived well. Farmhouses were simple buildings; townhouses had more rooms and were more luxurious.

Inside a Greek farmhouse

Read the descriptions of the parts of a farmhouse below, then fill in the labels.

Farmhouse features

- A **hearth** was used for cooking.
- The **dining area** had couches and tables for serving food.
- Every house had an **altar** where the family would offer sacrifices.
- The **porch** shaded the doorway. Its pillars were made from tree trunks.
- **Stone foundations** formed the solid basis of the house.
- **Window openings** had no glass but did have wooden shutters.
- The **roof** was made of clay tiles.
- **The women's quarters** (gynaeceum) upstairs often housed the weaving looms, babies' cradles, and couches.

What's the pot for?

The Greeks made huge amounts of pottery vases in different shapes for different tasks. The vases were made from high-quality clay and were often decorated with beautiful black or red paintings.

From the descriptions below, number the shape to match the task.

1. A pot used to mix wine and water, a calyx-krater, had two handles and a wide mouth.
2. A drinking cup, a skyphus, had a shallow bowl, two handles, and a wide mouth.
3. A storage container for wine or oil, an amphora, had a narrow mouth and neck and two handles.
4. A jug for pouring wine, an oenochoe, had one handle, a narrow neck, and a spout.

a.

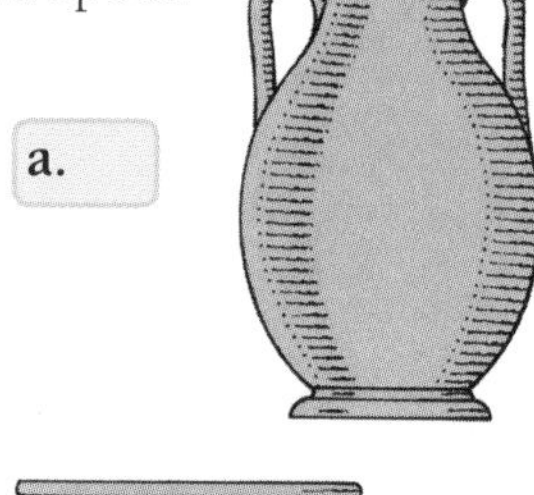

b.

c.

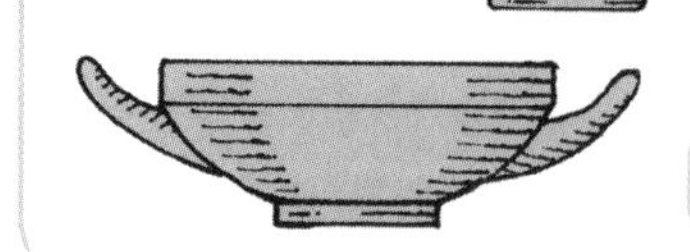

d.

Women's Lives

The lives of women in ancient Greece were fairly restricted. According to most male ancient Greek writers, a woman's place was in the home. However, upper-class women were known to take on roles as priestesses in the temples, and women in the countryside worked alongside their husbands in the fields.

Sappho

A female poet called Sappho lived on the island of Lesbos in the late seventh century BCE. Women in this part of Greece seem to have had more freedom than those in Athens. Sappho's beautiful poems give us a rare glimpse of their lives and their feelings.

True or false?

Check the boxes to show which of these statements are true or false. Use the information on this page to help you.

	TRUE	FALSE
1. Women had no place in religious festivals.	☐	☐
2. Women didn't get married until they were over 15.	☐	☐
3. Women could be small-scale market traders.	☐	☐
4. Women sat on councils and voted in assemblies.	☐	☐
5. Sappho was a poet from Lesbos.	☐	☐

Women fetching water from the well using special jars called amphorae

A woman's lot

- Girls married young, between the ages of 12 and 15.
- The main purpose for marriage was to have children.
- Women could be midwives, wet nurses, or market traders.
- Women had no place in assemblies or councils.
- In the home, women spun and wove wool into cloth.
- Water for the home was collected in jugs by women.

Weave your own cloth

Follow the steps below to create your own woven cloth. Vary colors and try different designs. You will need a ruler, pencil, hole punch, rectangle of card stock, string, and different colors of yarn.

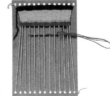

1 Use a ruler and pencil to mark out holes on a piece of card stock. Use the hole punch to make the holes.

2 Start in the top left corner and draw string through the holes to make straight lines on one side of the card stock.

3 Using a large needle, interweave different yarns through the string to create your design.

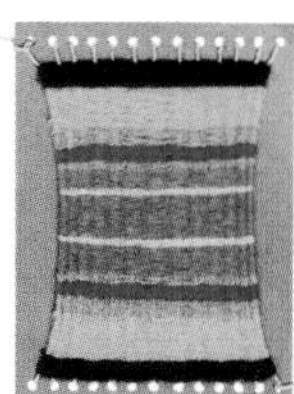

4 Tie each section of yarn neatly so that knots are tucked behind the front of your work.

Buying and Selling

For any society to work, there has to be trade. In ancient Greece, many people earned their living through their craft, such as blacksmiths, potters, sculptors, weavers, and farmers. All these people needed to show their wares and sell them. This was done in the city agora, or marketplace.

Athens agora quiz

People met in the agora to do business every day. It was also the political and legal heart of the city, surrounded by public buildings. These included law courts, meeting places for the council, and temples. There were also long colonnaded buildings, called stoa, which provided shade from the summer sun and shelter from rain, and were used for business.

Read the information on this page and on page 11 to answer the questions below.

Athens's agora in the 5th century BCE

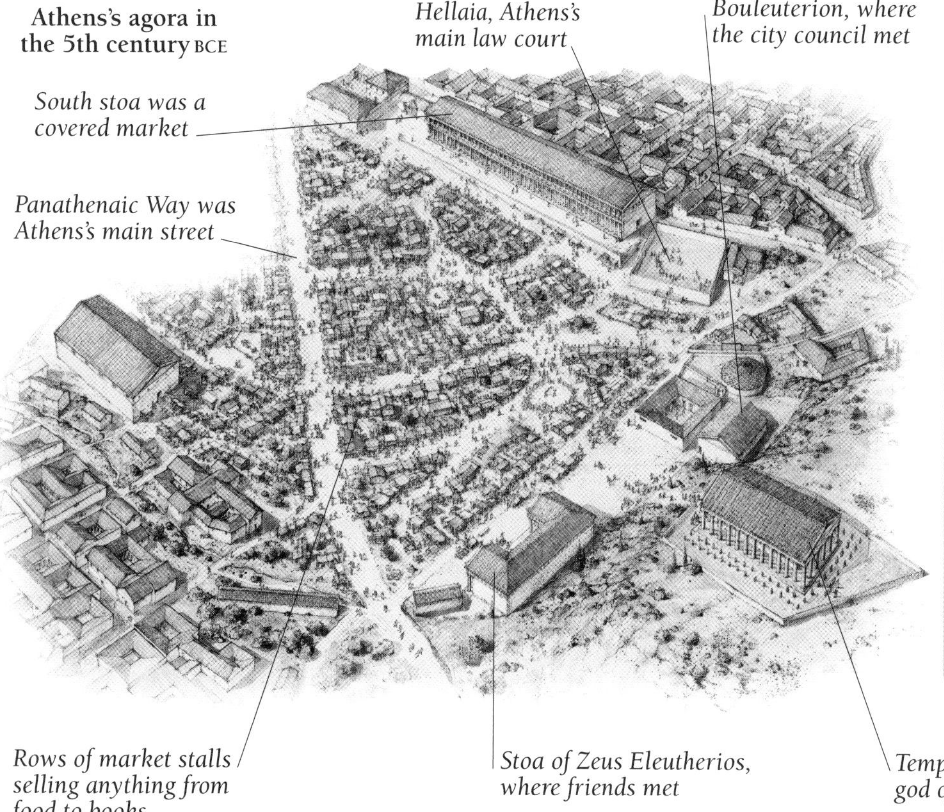

Hellaia, Athens's main law court

Bouleuterion, where the city council met

South stoa was a covered market

Panathenaic Way was Athens's main street

Rows of market stalls selling anything from food to books

Stoa of Zeus Eleutherios, where friends met

Temple of Hephaestus, god of metalworkers

1. What is the marketplace called?

....

2. What is the name for the colonnaded buildings used for business?

....

3. What was the main road through Athens?

....

4. Which god has a temple dedicated to him near the marketplace?

....

5. Which metal was so valuable to the Greeks that they melted down statues made from it to be used again?

....

Money

Athenian coin

Standard weights for coins began to be introduced throughout Greece in the sixth century BCE. A drachma was made from silver and weighed around 0.2 oz (4.3 g). Six obols made 1 drachma, 100 drachmas made 1 mina, and 60 mina was equal to 1 talent.

Imagine you were shopping for a feast. Here is a list of items you may want and their prices.

Price List

Bread, per loaf	**1 obol**
Olive oil, per gallon	**5 drachmas**
Lambs, each	**8 drachmas**
Honey, per pot	**9 obols**
Flour, per sack	**3 obols**
Lentils, per bag	**1 obol**
Pomegranates, per bag	**2 obols**

You need three loaves of bread, half a gallon of oil, and a lamb for a feast. How much do you spend?

....

A Greek Education

A boy born into a poor family had a very basic education and often followed his father into his trade. A boy from a rich family was sent to school at the age of 7. He learned reading, writing, math, literature, and music. Physical exercise was important for all boys and they went to the palaestra (wrestling ground) or the gymnasium to train. Girls were taught the skills they needed at home.

The ruins of a palaestra at Olympia

Greek writing

Try writing using the Greek alphabet. The first column of letters is capitals, the next is lowercase. C is written with a Kappa, F with a Phi, and J and Y with an Iota.

Your name: ....

Your nearest city: ....

Learning facts

- Boys were taught between the ages of 7 and 12.
- They were taken to school by a paedagogos, an enslaved person responsible for the boys' behavior.
- Some older boys were educated by sophists—men who were paid to teach a wide range of subjects.
- At the palaestra, boys played competitive games under the eye of a trainer called a paedotribe.
- Boys were taught running, jumping, wrestling, boxing, throwing the javelin, and discus. They were also taught to dance.
- They were taught music by a teacher called a kitharistes.

Learning puzzle

Draw a line to match the name to the job, using the facts above.

a. Sophist	1. He was in charge of the boys' behavior.
b. Kitharistes	2. He trained the boys in sports.
c. Paedotribe	3. He was paid a fee to teach a range of subjects.
d. Paedagogos	4. He taught music.

Boys learning to wrestle

Greek alphabet

Greek letter		Name	Equivalent
Α	α	Alpha	A
Β	β	Beta	B
Γ	γ	Gamma	G
Δ	δ	Delta	D
Ε	ϵ	Epsilon	E
Ζ	ζ	Zeta	Z
Η	η	Eta	E
Θ	θ	Theta	Th
Ι	ι	Iota	I
Κ	κ	Kappa	K
Λ	λ	Lambda	L
Μ	μ	Mu	M
Ν	ν	Nu	N
Ξ	ξ	Xi	X
Ο	ο	Omicron	O
Π	π	Pi	P
Ρ	ρ	Rho	R
Σ	σ	Sigma	S
Τ	τ	Tau	T
Υ	υ	Upsilon	U
Φ	ϕ	Phi	Ph
Χ	χ	Chi	Ch
Ψ	ψ	Psi	Ps
Ω	ω	Omega	O

Fun and Games

The ancient Greeks worked hard, but as they grew richer they also had time for fun. Men gathered in the evening for symposia, or wine-drinking parties. Men and women learned to dance and play music.

Greek musicians

A good symposium

For rich or poor, every symposium or dinner party followed formal rules. Wealthier hosts employed acrobats, musicians, and dancers as entertainment after their discussions.

Read through the following statements, then number them in the order in which they took place.

a. After the meal, guests washed their hands and were given a cup of wine.

b. Enslaved people greeted the guests at the door, then washed their hands and feet.

c. Often the evening ended with dancing and a komos—a rowdy procession through the streets!

Pipe player at a symposium

d. As they drank their wine, the master of ceremonies chose a subject for discussion.

e. Guests were shown to the andron (men's room) and lay down on couches, often two to a couch.

f. The first part of the evening was taken up with the meal, or deipnon. While eating they did not drink.

Instruments today

Which of these instruments descend directly from those played by the ancient Greeks? Using the pictures and text on this page and on page 12, put a check by those that do.

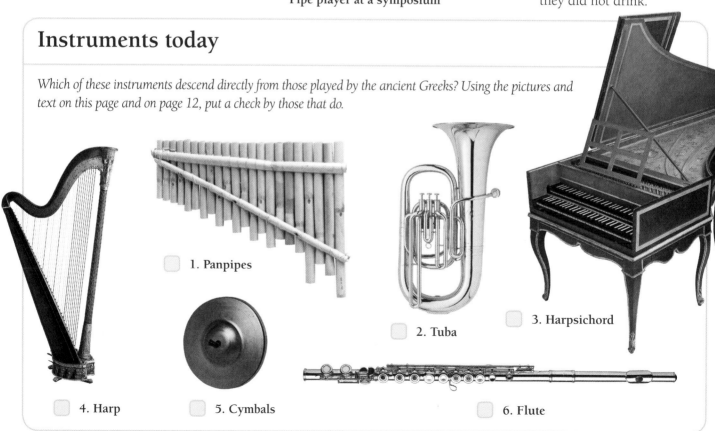

1. Panpipes

2. Tuba

3. Harpsichord

4. Harp

5. Cymbals

6. Flute

Wining and Dining

Women and enslaved people in a Greek household were responsible for preparing and cooking food. At a symposium, several dishes were served to the men on small tables placed in front of the couches. Dishes were simple, such as bean soup, cheese, olives, grilled fish, and pork sausages.

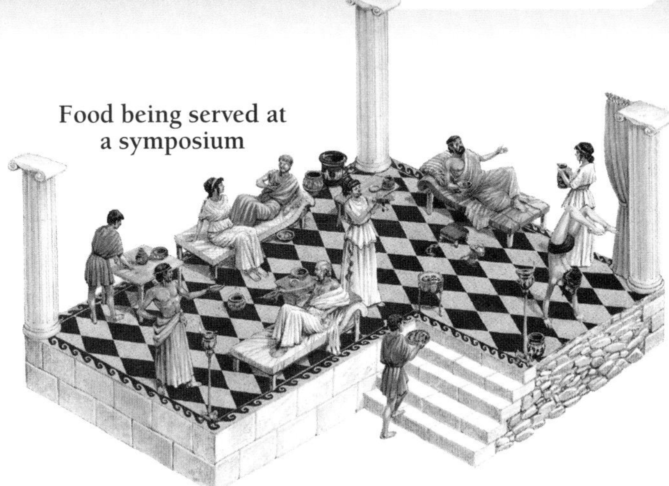
Food being served at a symposium

What did they eat?

All the food below is available in Greece today. Foods that the ancient Greeks ate are in the column on the left. However, foods on the right were not available to the ancient Greeks—they came from the Americas and did not reach Europe until many centuries later.

Draw pictures of the missing food to fill in the gaps in both columns.

Food available in ancient Greece:

Food not available:

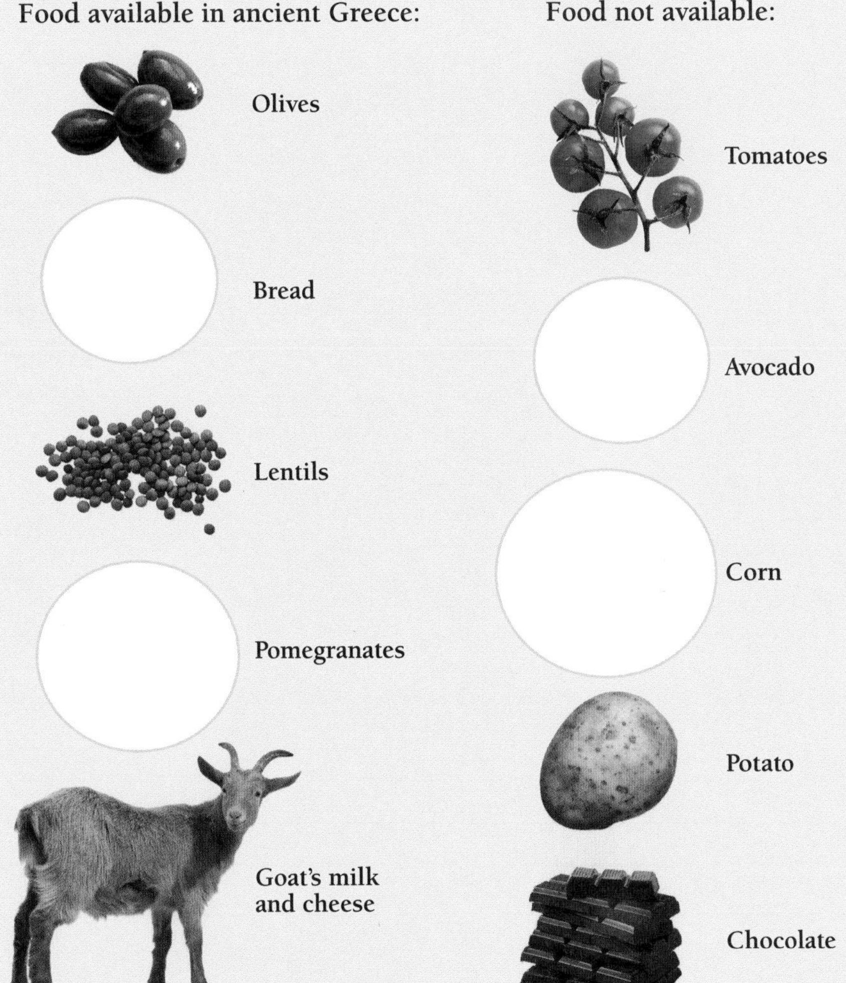

Greek honey fritters

Ingredients

- *1 cup (120g) all-purpose flour*
- *1 cup (225ml) water*
- *4 teaspoons honey*
- *Oil for frying*
- *2 tablespoons (15g) sesame seeds*

Honey

Sesame seeds

1 Mix the flour, water, and 2 teaspoons of honey to make a dough.

2 Heat 4 teaspoons of oil in a frying pan and pour in ¼ of the dough.

3 When it thickens, turn it over 2 to 3 times to fry it on both sides.

4 Prepare 3 more fritters in the same way.

5 Serve them warm on a plate, pour over the rest of the honey, and sprinkle toasted sesame seeds over them. Enjoy!

WARNING Make sure you have an adult to help you. The oil is hot.

Greek Theater

Many words that we use to describe elements of the theater—including drama, scene, comedy, and tragedy—come from Greek. This is because the Greeks invented theater in Athens over 2,500 years ago.

A Greek play

At the theater

Greek theaters were always built in a semi-circle. They were open air and set into a hillside with fantastic views of the countryside behind the stage.

The picture shows an aerial view of a theater. Read the description of a theater, then add the labels to the picture.

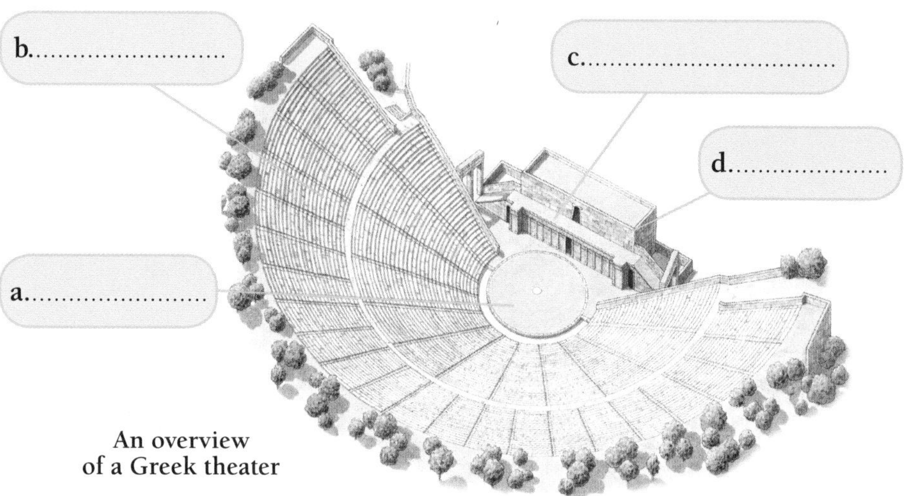

An overview of a Greek theater

All the world's a stage

Greek plays had certain rules. There were just two forms of play—tragedy and comedy. All the actors were men. They wore masks with exaggerated expressions. The play had a chorus—a few actors who sang and danced. Plays began with a prologue and ended with an exodus sung by the chorus.

Answer these questions using the information on this page, on page 12, and the charts at the back of the book to help you.

1. In what season did the festival of the Dionysia take place?

....

2. What is the name of the group of actors who sang and danced?

....

3. Where did the audience sit?

....

4. Who was the founder of comedy?

....

5. What started a Greek play?

....

Theater facts

- The circular **orchestra** in the center was used for dancing and singing, often performed by a chorus.
- The actors performed on a **stage**, which was a raised platform above the orchestra.
- The building behind the stage was called the **skene**. It had at least one doorway through which the actors could enter and exit. It was decorated to suit the play being performed.
- Passageways, called **paradoi**, from the sides on to the stage and orchestra were used by the actors and by the audience when they wanted to enter or leave the theater.
- The sloping viewing area was called the **theatron**. The seats were the stone steps, and viewers would bring their own cushions.

Did you know?

The playwright Sophocles decided to paint the skene with images from nature to suit a play he was presenting. This started the art of theater scenery.

Clothing and Beauty

Greek clothes were simply made and easy to wear and store. They were not fitted, but made from rectangles of fabric drawn to the body with a belt. Women had long hair, which they curled and held in place with scented wax and oils. Cloth hair bands were also popular.

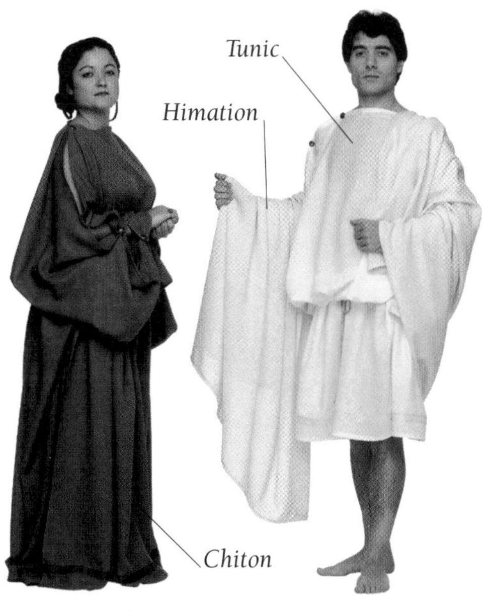

Make your own chiton

To learn how simple it was to make a Greek tunic, follow the instructions below. You will need: an old rectangular bed sheet, safety pins, string or rope, and some scissors. Ask an adult for advice before you start.

1 Fold the sheet in half widthwise and then cut along the fold.

2 Place the two pieces together and start to fasten one end together using safety pins.

3 Make sure that gaps are left between each pin and that a large gap is left for the head.

4 Place the fastened fabric over the head and use the rope or string to gather the chiton in around the waist.

Did you know?

Perfume was made by mixing different items with oil. Those used most often included cinnamon, basil, almonds, roses, lavender, and lilies.

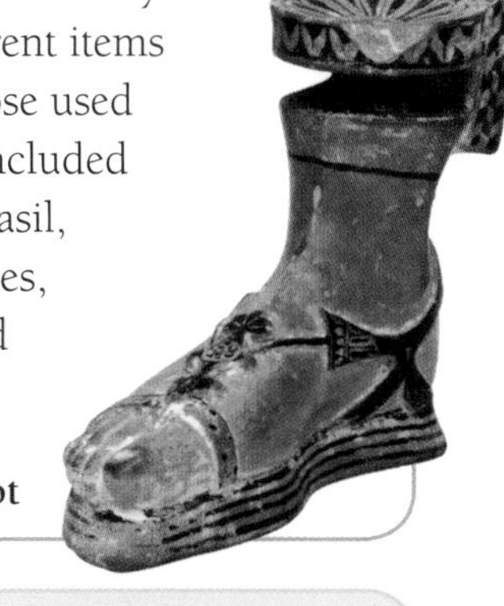

Perfume pot

Greek fabric

Greek women wove cloth at home, but were also able to buy it at the agora, or marketplace. More elaborate, colored cloth was bought by the wealthy and was decorated with designs around the border.

Read the information on this page and on page 10 and check the fabrics that were not used in Greek times.

☐ Silk

☐ Linen

☐ Denim

☐ Velvet

☐ Wool

The Scholars

The Greeks searched for answers to the big questions of existence. They called their study of the universe and the meaning of human behavior philosophy. Greek thinkers studied science, mathematics, politics, geography, and more. They still influence western ideas today.

Socrates

Pythagorean theorem

In the 6th century BCE, Pythagoras of Samos believed that everything in the universe could be explained by numbers. He searched for patterns of numbers in all things.

Look at this shape. Inside is a triangle with horizontal and vertical sides. Where they meet is a right angle (90°).

1. Count the yellow squares in the block below the horizontal line.

   ....

2. Count the red squares in the block next to the vertical line.

   ....

3. Add these two numbers together.

   ....

4. Now count how many red and yellow squares there are in the square next to the diagonal line.

   ....

5. What do you notice about the last two answers?

   ....

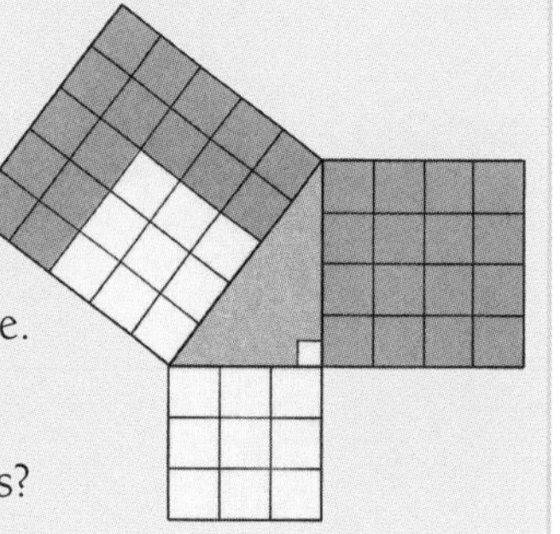

What's the big idea?

Ancient philosophers came up with ideas on what the universe is made from. From the information on this page link the philosopher to what he thought the made up the universe.

1. Thales
2. Heraclitus
3. Democritus

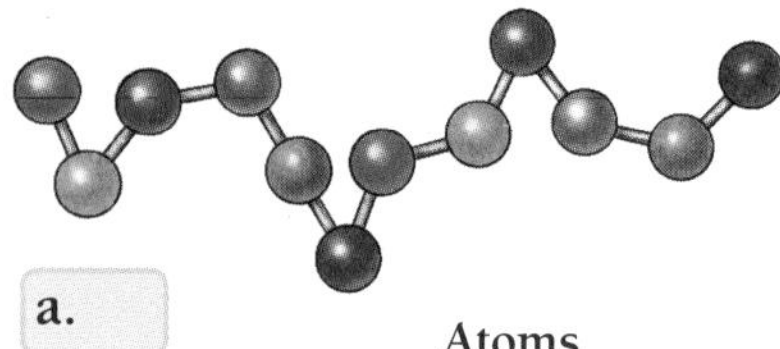
a.

Atoms

b.

Fire

c.

Water

Greek philosophers' facts

- Thales of Miletus was the first known Greek philosopher—his teachings date from 580 BCE. He believed the universe was made up of water.
- Writing in about 500 BCE, Heraclitus of Ephesus thought the universe was made from fire. He thought everything was in constant movement, like a river.
- Democritus of Abdera lived in the late 5th century BCE. He argued that the universe was endless and made up of tiny particles called atoms.
- Socrates (c. 469–399 BCE) enjoyed exploring moral issues. He discussed truth, beauty, and goodness and what they meant.
- Plato (c. 429–347 BCE), Socrates' greatest follower, studied how people acted in society and founded the Greek Academy.
- Aristotle (384–322 BCE) studied with Plato and was interested in science, politics, and logic. He taught Alexander the Great.

Plato

Science and Medicine

Greek scientists were influenced by Egyptian and Babylonian scholars. They made great advances in science, and particularly in medicine. The Greeks believed illness was sent as a punishment from the gods. Asclepius, the god of medicine, would help his priests give cures. The priests' work began progress toward the practice of modern medicine.

The god Asclepius

True or false?

Check the boxes to show which of these statements are true or false, using the information on this page to help you.

	TRUE	FALSE
1. The god of medicine was called Asclepius.	☐	☐
2. Hippocrates is the founder of modern medicine.	☐	☐
3. Hippocrates' school of medicine was in Crete.	☐	☐
4. The Hippocratic Oath was a list of illnesses.	☐	☐
5. The writings of Hippocrates are called the *Corpus*.	☐	☐

Hippocrates

Hippocrates (c. 469–399 BCE) is often described as the founder of modern medicine. He believed that all illnesses had natural causes. He aimed to do away with the superstitious beliefs that illnesses were sent by gods.

- He based his treatments on detailed observations of patients' symptoms.
- He wrote 53 books on medical topics, now known as the *Corpus*.
- He created a code for the way doctors should behave, which has become known as the Hippocratic Oath.
- He set up a school of medicine on the island of Cos.
- He taught that the human body was a single organism and that each part could only be understood as part of the whole.

Hippocrates

Eureka!

Archimedes (287–211 BCE), a brilliant scientist and inventor, made a great discovery when getting into his bath. He noticed that the level of water went up as he got in. He realized that you could measure how much space an object took up (its volume) by placing it in water. It was said he was so excited about this that he ran naked through the streets, yelling "Eureka!" ("I've found it!")

Figure out the volume of your hand by using the same method. You will need a jar, a bowl, water, and a measuring jug.

1 Fill a jar to the very top with water and place it in the bowl.

2 Put your hand slowly into the jar and watch the water spill over into the bowl.

3 Take your hand out of the jar and pour the water from the bowl into the measuring jug. The amount of water that spilled over is the volume of your hand.

Olympic Games

When the Olympic games were on, thousands of men and boys from all over the Greek world gathered in a temporary encampment at Olympia to take part and watch.

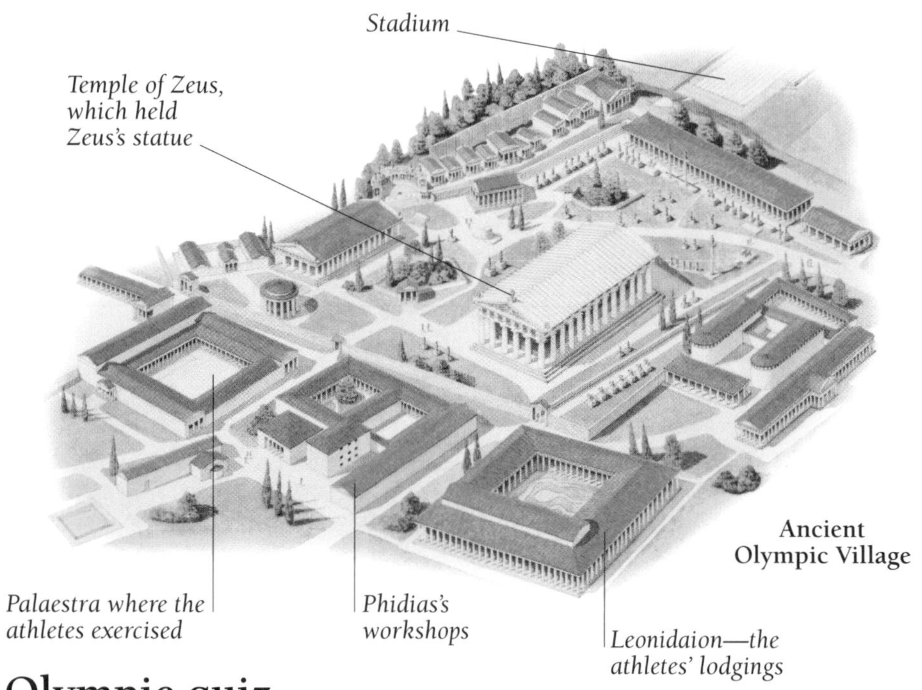

Olympic facts

- The day before the games, the Olympic festival began with a religious procession to Zeus's statue in his temple.
- Zeus's statue designed by Phidias was later named one of the Seven Wonders of the Ancient World.
- The games included chariot racing and the pentathlon, which involved the five sports of running, throwing the discus and javelin, wrestling, and the long jump.
- On the third and fourth days, boxers, runners, and wrestlers competed and there was a race with runners wearing armor.
- The last day was prize-giving and a victors' banquet.

Olympic quiz

Read the information on this page and on page 12 to answer the questions below.

1. How often were the Olympic games held?

....

2. What were the games seen as a training for?

....

3. How many sports did pentathletes perform?

....

4. When did the ancient Olympic games stop taking place?

....

Ancient influence

*Modern games still show the influence of the sports practiced by the ancient Greeks. Look at the photographs below, then check the boxes that show sports the Greeks **did not** do.*

☐ a. Javelin

☐ b. High jump

☐ c. Skiing

☐ d. Running

☐ e. Swimming

☐ f. Long jump

A Hoplite's Life

Warfare was part of Greek life. If the city-states weren't fighting each other, they were defending themselves against the Persians. The Greek soldier was called a hoplite from the Greek word *hoplon*, meaning equipment. Each hoplite had to pay for his own weapons and armor.

Name the hoplite's gear

Label the different parts of the hoplite's armor using the information on this page. Choose from:

cuirass	**xiphos**
greaves	**helmet**
aspis	**tunic**
sandals	

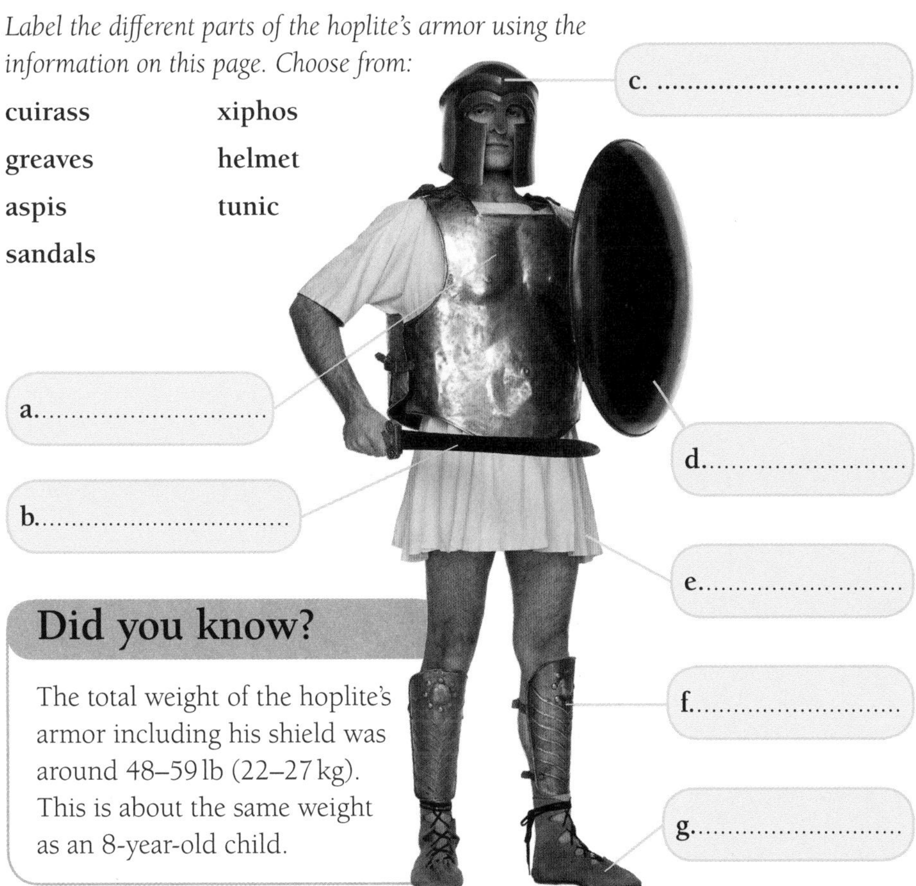

Did you know?

The total weight of the hoplite's armor including his shield was around 48–59 lb (22–27 kg). This is about the same weight as an 8-year-old child.

Fighting facts

- Campaigns usually took place in the summer when the weather was better.
- Spartan hoplites trained from childhood to become exceptional fighters. They were the only Greek soldiers to earn permanent wages.
- A hoplite usually wore a tunic over which was a bronze breastplate called a cuirass. He wore metal shin guards called greaves.
- To protect their heads, hoplites wore helmets. Sometimes these had crests of horse hair to make the wearer look frightening.
- A hoplite carried a spear—the most common being a doru—and a wooden shield called an aspis. Often he also had a short sword known as a xiphos.
- Battles rarely lasted more than an hour. After an initial clash, each army would try to break the line of the other in a pushing match. Once lines were broken, soldiers often fled the field.

Design your own shield

The shield was 3 ft 3 in (1 m) wide and sometimes decorated, either with a design that showed where the fighter came from or with something personal to the carrier. Spartans used a red capital lambda (the Greek letter L), while Athenians painted a little owl, and the Thebans a sphinx.

Design your own shield here, with either something Greek or something that is important to you.

Sea Battles

Greek city-states were spread not just around the Aegean Sea but also the Mediterranean, on the mainland, and on islands. This meant sea travel was vitally important. The Greeks were great sailors and sea warriors. Greek warships such as the trireme—meaning three rows of oars—were sleek, fast, and effective.

Did you know?

Triremes were used by Greeks, Phoenicians, and later Romans. According to Thucydides, they were introduced to Greece by the Corinthians in the 8th century BCE.

Cross-section of the trireme

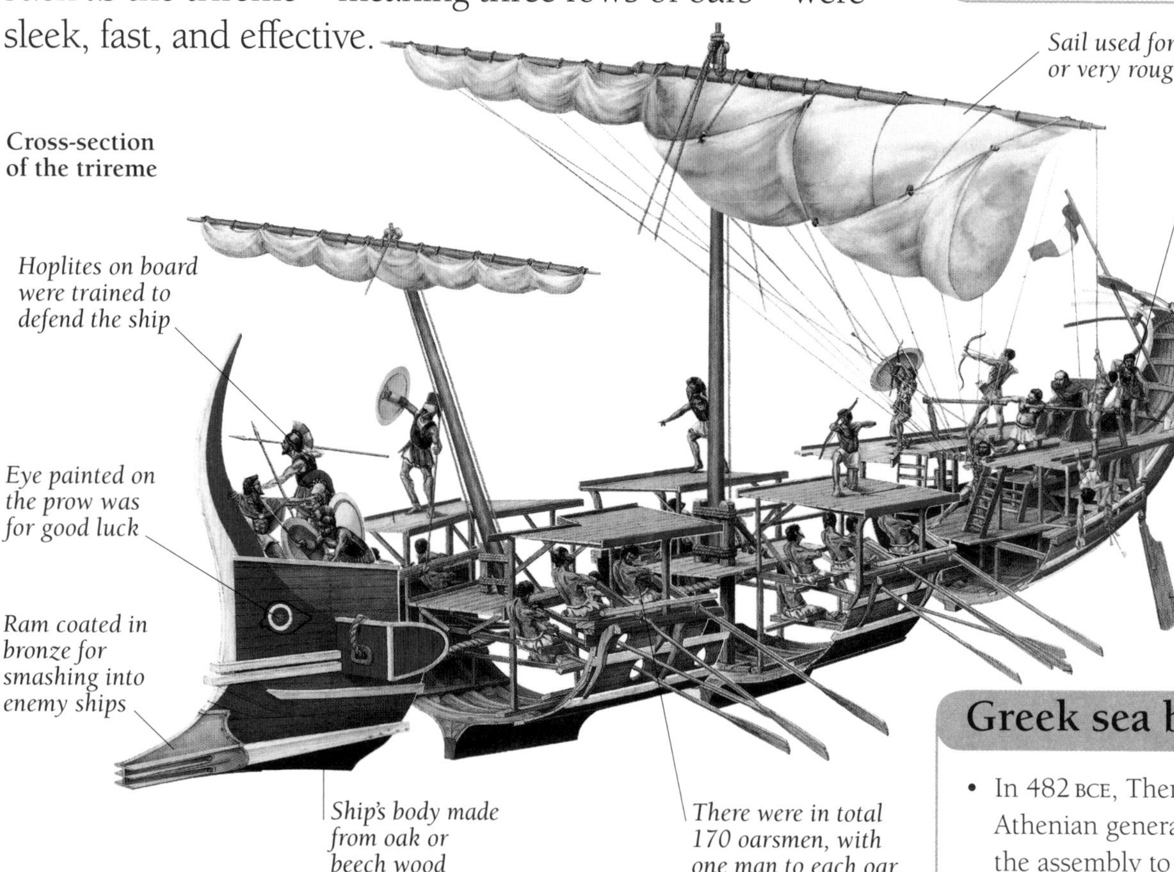
Sail used for long journeys or very rough seas
The trierarch was the captain who owned the ship and paid all the costs.
Hoplites on board were trained to defend the ship
Eye painted on the prow was for good luck
Shorter oars at end of ship
Ram coated in bronze for smashing into enemy ships
Ship's body made from oak or beech wood
There were in total 170 oarsmen, with one man to each oar.

Trireme test

Use the information on this page and on page 18 to answer these questions

1. What does the word trireme mean?
   ....
2. How many oarsmen were there?
   ....
3. Who owned the trireme?
   ....
4. Why was an eye painted on the ship?
   ....
5. Which metal was used on the ram?
   ....
6. Which Persian king was defeated at Salamis?
   ....
7. Which war started in 431 BCE?
   ....
8. How many Spartan ships were lost at Arginusae?
   ....

Greek sea battles

- In 482 BCE, Themistocles, an Athenian general, persuaded the assembly to spend money on a vast fleet of 200 triremes. This idea gave Athens great power in the Aegean.
- Sparta challenged Athens's supremacy in 431 BCE, starting the Peloponnesian War, which lasted over 20 years.
- In 406 BCE the Arginusae battle lasted all day and resulted in 75 Spartan ships and 25 Athenian ships being destroyed.
- In the battle at Aegospotami in 404 BCE, Spartan commander Lysander led his side to victory, finally destroying the last of the Athenian fleet.

Alexander the Great

In just 13 years, from the moment he became king of Macedonia to when he died, Alexander won dozens of battles and over 20 sieges. He was one of the greatest generals the world has ever known. He also found time to found new cities on his travels.

Alexander's campaigns

The following pictures and captions tell the story of Alexander's rule. Number them in the correct order, starting with the earliest event. Use the Alexander facts to help you.

a. The Greek city of Thebes rebelled against Alexander. Alexander swiftly ransacked the city and burned it to the ground. After this there was no more Greek rebellion and Alexander was in control.

d. Darius III of Persia and Alexander met in battle at Issus. Darius made a mistake in choosing to fight on a narrow plain. This meant his vast army had to stand one behind the other which led to huge casualties. Alexander was victorious, but Darius escaped.

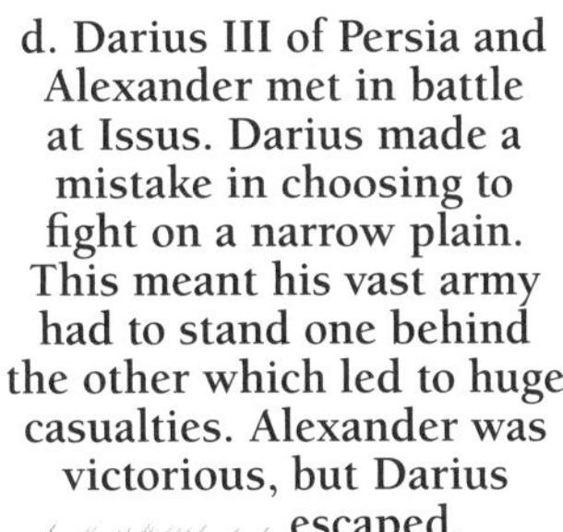

b. Alexander was planning to invade Arabia and then the coast of North Africa, but a fever struck him down. He continued to order his men from his sickbed, but on June 10, 323 BCE he died. He was just 32 years old.

c. Philip of Macedonia was murdered, leaving 20-year-old Alexander to lead the country. The first thing Alexander had to do was win over the loyalty of the army.

e. Alexander marched on to Egypt, a jewel in the Persian Empire. The Egyptians hated the Persians and welcomed Alexander warmly. He became king, or pharaoh, and started to build the great city of Alexandria.

f. In order to defeat the Persian fleet Alexander decided to take control of Mediterranean ports. If the fleet could not land to take on food, they would have to surrender. The people of the port of Tyre tried to resist, but after seven months Alexander's forces captured the city.

Alexander facts

- Alexander was born in Macedonia, in 356 BCE. His father was Philip, the king.
- After Philip's murder in 336 BCE, Alexander became king.
- In 335 BCE Alexander crushed the Greek city of Thebes.
- Alexander defeated Darius at the Battle of Issus in 333 BCE.
- Along the Mediterranean coast, Alexander won the siege of Tyre in 332 BCE. Later in the same year he was recognized as king of Egypt.
- He defeated Darius at the battle of Gaugamela in 331 BCE.
- Alexander started his invasion of India in 327 BCE.
- He died, possibly of malaria, in 323 BCE.

g. Alexander and Darius met again in battle at Gaugamela to decide the fate of the Persian empire. Alexander found a way through the Persian army's defenses to the king himself. Again, Darius fled. The empire was now Alexander's.

h. Alexander turned his attention to unknown lands, heading into India. However, Alexander's soldiers refused to continue. Eventually Alexander gave in to his men and started to lead them back.

History of Ancient Greece

Check or number the boxes to answer each question. Check your answers on page 46.

1 Number the following Greek Ages in order, from the earliest to the latest:

- ☐ a. Classical Age
- ☐ b. Dark Age
- ☐ c. Hellenistic Age
- ☐ d. Bronze Age

2 When did the Minoans reach the height of their power?

- ☐ a. Between 2500 and 2000 BCE
- ☐ b. Between 2000 and 1500 BCE
- ☐ c. Between 1500 and 1000 BCE
- ☐ d. Between 1000 and 500 BCE

3 Which ancient settlement did Sir Arthur Evans discover on Crete?

- ☐ a. Athens
- ☐ b. Sparta
- ☐ c. Mycenae
- ☐ d. Knossos

4 Who was said to have rescued Ariadne from the Minotaur?

- ☐ a. Perseus
- ☐ b. Theseus
- ☐ c. Minos
- ☐ d. Prometheus

5 Where was Mycenae?

- ☐ a. Crete
- ☐ b. The Greek mainland
- ☐ c. Rhodes
- ☐ d. Corfu

6 Who found the famous "mask of Agamemnon"?

- ☐ a. Sir Arthur Evans
- ☐ b. Howard Carter
- ☐ c. Heinrich Schliemann
- ☐ d. James Cook

7 Who is said to have written the epic poem about the Trojan wars?

- ☐ a. Aeschylus
- ☐ b. Aristophanes
- ☐ c. Socrates
- ☐ d. Euripides
- ☐ e. Homer

8 Check the elements essential for creating an early Greek city-state:

- ☐ a. Supply of fresh water
- ☐ b. Good neighbors
- ☐ c. Land to grow food
- ☐ d. Enslaved people
- ☐ e. Mountains to hide in

9 Why did Greeks call foreigners barbarians?

- ☐ a. Because they were fierce
- ☐ b. Because they were like sheep
- ☐ c. Because their language sounded like "bar bar" to the Greeks

10 Who united the whole of Greece at the start of the Hellenistic age?

- ☐ a. Themistocles
- ☐ b. Philip of Macedonia
- ☐ c. Alexander the Great
- ☐ d. Aristotle

Cities and Rulers

Check or number the boxes to answer each question. Check your answers on page 46.

1 Which was the largest and richest city-state on mainland Greece?

- a. Thebes
- b. Corinth
- c. Sparta
- d. Athens
- e. Delphi

2 What kind of government did Athens establish after 510 BCE?

- a. Tyranny
- b. Monarchy
- c. Democracy
- d. Oligarchy

3 How often did the Athenian Assembly take place?

- a. Every week
- b. Every other day
- c. Every nine days
- d. Every month

4 Which city's emblem was the winged horse?

- a. Corinth
- b. Sparta
- c. Thebes
- d. Athens

5 What city did Greeks visit to consult the oracles?

- a. Corinth
- b. Sparta
- c. Thebes
- d. Delphi
- e. Athens

6 In times of war who made the decisions in Athens?

- a. Ecclesia
- b. Strategi
- c. Elders of the tribes
- d. Council members

7 In Sparta, who limited the powers of the kings?

- a. The citizens
- b. The Assembly
- c. The ephors
- d. The queens
- e. The princes

8 During the Persian wars, who led the victory against the Persians at Marathon?

- a. Xerxes
- b. Miltiades
- c. Pericles
- d. Thucydides

9 In 482 BCE, who persuaded Athens to spend money on a vast fleet of 200 triremes?

- a. Perseus
- b. Cleisthenes
- c. Hippias
- d. Themistocles

10 Who instructed the rebuilding of the Parthenon after the Persian wars?

- a. Minos
- b. Hippias
- c. Pericles
- d. Plato

Greek Religion

Check or number the boxes to answer each question. Check your answers on page 46.

1 Where did the Greeks believe their gods lived?

- [ ] **a.** In the sky
- [ ] **b.** At Mount Olympus
- [ ] **c.** At Delphi
- [ ] **d.** In the sea

2 Zeus was thought to be god of what?

- [ ] **a.** Oceans
- [ ] **b.** Land
- [ ] **c.** Weather
- [ ] **d.** Mountains

3 Who was the god of the underworld?

- [ ] **a.** Poseidon
- [ ] **b.** Aphrodite
- [ ] **c.** Apollo
- [ ] **d.** Hades
- [ ] **e.** Demeter

4 Which Greek god crossed the sky every day?

- [ ] **a.** Hera
- [ ] **b.** Hephaestus
- [ ] **c.** Apollo
- [ ] **d.** Persephone

5 Who was given twelve labors by the king Eurystheus?

- [ ] **a.** Prometheus
- [ ] **b.** Theseus
- [ ] **c.** Hercules
- [ ] **d.** Hippolyte
- [ ] **d.** Diomedes

6 What is a temenos?

- [ ] **a.** A temple
- [ ] **b.** An altar
- [ ] **c.** An sacrifice
- [ ] **d.** A sanctuary

7 Check all the materials temples were built from.

- [ ] **a.** Slate
- [ ] **b.** Marble
- [ ] **c.** Granite
- [ ] **d.** Limestone
- [ ] **e.** Wood

8 Which style of temple column is decorated with a scroll-like design?

- [ ] **a.** Corinthian
- [ ] **b.** Ionic
- [ ] **c.** Doric

9 How did wealthy Greek people mark the grave of their dead?

- [ ] **a.** With a stone stele
- [ ] **b.** With a wooden cross
- [ ] **c.** With a temple
- [ ] **d.** With a tent

10 Who rows the dead across the river Styx?

- [ ] **a.** Hermes
- [ ] **b.** Hades
- [ ] **c.** Charon
- [ ] **d.** Demeter

Daily Life

Check or number the boxes to answer each question. Check your answers on page 46.

1 Check the item a Greek home did not have.

- ☐ **a.** Window
- ☐ **b.** Porch
- ☐ **c.** Carpet
- ☐ **d.** Stairs
- ☐ **e.** Door

2 What were roof tiles made from?

- ☐ **a.** Straw
- ☐ **b.** Clay
- ☐ **c.** Wood
- ☐ **d.** Slate

3 What were the women's quarters in the home called?

- ☐ **a.** Gynaeceum
- ☐ **b.** Ecclesia
- ☐ **c.** Symposium
- ☐ **d.** Strategi

4 Check the foods that the ancient Greeks did not eat.

- ☐ **a.** Potatoes
- ☐ **b.** Lentils
- ☐ **c.** Tomatoes
- ☐ **d.** Olives

5 Where was the cooking done?

- ☐ **a.** In an oven
- ☐ **b.** On an open hearth
- ☐ **c.** In a fireplace
- ☐ **d.** On a stove

6 What were most Greek clothes made from?

- ☐ **a.** Silk
- ☐ **b.** Velvet
- ☐ **c.** Denim
- ☐ **d.** Wool

7 What is a himation?

- ☐ **a.** A man's cloak
- ☐ **b.** A woman's dress
- ☐ **c.** A child's tunic
- ☐ **d.** A handbag

8 When did Greek women usually get married?

- ☐ **a.** Between 18 and 20
- ☐ **b.** Between 16 and 18
- ☐ **c.** Between 20 and 22
- ☐ **d.** Between 12 and 15

9 What might boys learn to do in a palaestra?

- ☐ **a.** Read
- ☐ **b.** Write
- ☐ **c.** Wrestle
- ☐ **d.** Sing

10 Who taught boys music?

- ☐ **a.** A kitharistes
- ☐ **b.** A paedagogos
- ☐ **c.** A sophist
- ☐ **d.** A paedotribe

11 What are the first and last letters of the Greek alphabet?

- ☐ **a.** Beta and Gamma
- ☐ **b.** Rho and Tau
- ☐ **c.** Alpha and Omega
- ☐ **d.** Sigma and Psi

Entertainment

Check or number the boxes to answer each question. Check your answers on page 46.

1 What did a Greek play end with?

- a. Orchestra
- b. Prologue
- c. Chorus
- d. Exodus

2 When did the drama competitions during the festival of Dionysus start?

- a. Fourth century BCE
- b. Fifth century BCE
- c. Sixth century BCE
- d. Seventh century BCE

3 What was the name of the building behind the stage?

- a. Theatron
- b. Orchestra
- c. Paradoi
- d. Skene

4 Who is considered the father of comedy?

- a. Sophocles
- b. Aristophanes
- c. Euripides
- d. Aeschylus

5 How often did the Olympics take place?

- a. Every summer
- b. Every other year
- c. Every four years
- d. Every ten years

6 What did the games start with?

- a. A procession to the temple of Zeus
- b. A wrestling display
- c. A procession of each country's athletes
- d. A circus

7 What were Olympic winners given?

- a. A gold medal
- b. A laurel wreath
- c. A bag of money
- d. A horse

8 Which instruments did the Greeks play?

- a. Pan pipes
- b. Harp
- c. Violin
- d. Piano
- e. Cymbals

9 Check all the entertainments there were at a symposium.

- a. Dancing
- b. Singing
- c. Wrestling
- d. Drinking
- e. Discussion

Greeks at Work

Check or number the boxes to answer each question. Check your answers on page 46.

1 Where in the city did people sell their wares?

- ☐ **a.** The stoa
- ☐ **b.** The bouleuterion
- ☐ **c.** The Hellaia
- ☐ **d.** The agora

2 Which metal was used most frequently by the Greeks?

- ☐ **a.** Bronze
- ☐ **b.** Silver
- ☐ **c.** Gold
- ☐ **d.** Tin

3 How many obols made a drachma?

- ☐ **a.** Three
- ☐ **b.** Six
- ☐ **c.** Ten
- ☐ **d.** Twenty

4 Which city-state was the only one to pay their soldiers permanent wages?

- ☐ **a.** Athens
- ☐ **b.** Corinth
- ☐ **c.** Sparta
- ☐ **d.** Thebes

5 What could a slave save up to buy?

- ☐ **a.** A house
- ☐ **b.** Freedom
- ☐ **c.** A goat
- ☐ **d.** Some land

6 Which of these farm animals was most common?

- ☐ **a.** Cows
- ☐ **b.** Sheep
- ☐ **c.** Goats
- ☐ **d.** Pigs

7 What did farmers build to help grow olive trees?

- ☐ **a.** Sloping fields
- ☐ **b.** Flat terraces
- ☐ **c.** Stone walls
- ☐ **d.** Glasshouses

8 Who was the earliest known Greek philosopher?

- ☐ **a.** Heraclitus of Ephesus
- ☐ **b.** Socrates
- ☐ **c.** Aristotle
- ☐ **d.** Thales of Miletus

9 Who was the founder of modern medicine?

- ☐ **a.** Asclepius
- ☐ **b.** Dionysus
- ☐ **c.** Hippocrates
- ☐ **d.** Pericles

10 Check those things the famous sculptor Phidias designed and created?

- ☐ **a.** The Parthenon
- ☐ **b.** Mycenae
- ☐ **c.** Delphi
- ☐ **d.** Zeus's statue at Olympia

Activity Answers

Once you have completed each page of activities, check your answers below.

Page 14
Where's where?

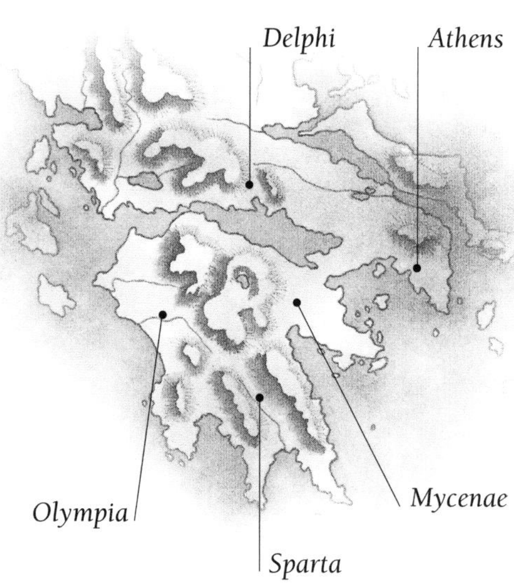

Page 14
Fill in the dates

Bronze Age	2900–1200 BCE
Dark Age	1200–800 BCE
Archaic Age	800–500 BCE
Classical Age	500–323 BCE
Hellenistic Age	323–31 BCE

Page 15
Theseus and the Minotaur

1 Crete
2 14
3 Half-man, half-bull
4 Ariadne
5 A sword and a ball of wool
6 Naxos

Page 16
A view of Mycenae

1 City walls
2 Lion's Gate
3 Grave circle
4 Great ramp
5 King's palace

Page 17
Who's on which side?

GREEKS	TROJANS
1 Menelaus	**1** Paris
2 Agamemnon	**2** Hector
3 Achilles	**3** Priam
4 Patroclus	**4** Cassandra
5 Odysseus	**5** Aeneas

Page 17
Odysseus and Polyphemus quiz

1 Polyphemus
2 Cyclops
3 Wine
4 Eye
5 Sheep

Page 18
Fill in the dates

1 479 BCE
2 490 BCE
3 480 BCE
4 499 BCE
5 480 BCE
6 480 BCE

Page 18
The Parthenon

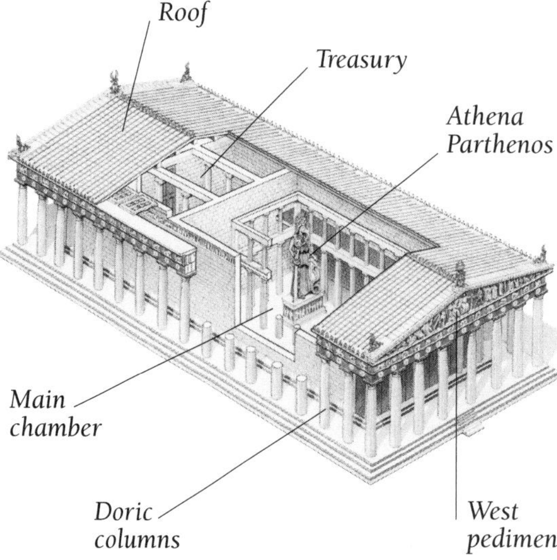

Page 19
Democracy quiz

1 500
2 101–1,001
3 10
4 6,000
5 Every nine days

Page 19
Famous Athenians

a 4
b 1
c 2
d 3
e 5

Page 20
Greek gods' family tree

1 Rhea
2 Athena
3 Persephone
4 Hera
5 Apollo
6 Poseidon

Page 20
Match the gods with nature

1 Artemis
2 Poseidon
3 Apollo
4 Hephaestus
5 Zeus

Page 21
The twelve labors of Hercules

a 6
b 4
c 1

Page 21
Perseus and Medusa the Gorgon

1 Polydectes
2 Medusa
3 A polished shield
4 Hermes
5 In a bag

Page 22
Temple of Artemis at Ephesus
a 3
b 5
c 6
d 1
e 4
f 2

Page 22
Spot the column
a 3
b 1
c 2

Page 23
Funeral rites
a 3
b 4
c 1
d 5
e 6
f 2

Page 23
Hades and Persephone
1 Underworld
2 Zeus
3 Demeter
4 Crops
5 Spring and summer

Page 24
Inside a Greek farmhouse
a Roof
b Women's quarters
c Window opening
d Dining area
e Hearth
f Altar
g Stone foundations
h Porch

Page 24
What's the pot for?
a 3 **c** 4
b 1 **d** 2

Page 25
True or false?
1 False
2 False
3 True
4 False
5 True

Page 26
Athens' agora facts
1 Agora
2 Stoa
3 Panathenaic Way
4 Hephaestus
5 Bronze

Page 26
Money
11 drachmas or 66 obols

Page 27
Learning puzzle
a 3
b 4
c 2
d 1

Page 28
A good symposium
a 4
b 1
c 6
d 5
e 2
f 3

Page 28
Instruments today
1 Panpipes
4 Harp
5 Cymbals
6 Flute

Page 30
At the theater
a Orchestra
b Theatron
c Stage
d Skene

Page 30
All the world's a stage
1 Spring
2 Chorus
3 Theatron
4 Aristophanes
5 Prologue

Page 31
Greek fabric
Denim and velvet

Page 32
Pythagorean theorem
1 9
2 16
3 25
4 25
5 They are the same
Pythagoras noticed that for every right-angled triangle, whatever its size, the answers to the questions 3 and 4 were ALWAYS the same. He wrote "The square on the hypotenuse (diagonal line) is equal to the sum (total) of the squares on the other two sides."

Page 32
What's the big idea?
a 3 **b** 2 **c** 1

Page 33
True or false?
1 True **4** False
2 True **5** True
3 False

Page 34
Olympic quiz
1 Every four years
2 Warfare
3 5
4 Late 4th century CE

Page 34
Ancient influence
b, c, and e

Page 35
Name the hoplite's kit
a cuirass
b xiphos
c helmet
d aspis
e tunic
f greaves
g sandals

Page 36
Trireme test
1 Three rows of oars
2 170
3 Trierarch
4 For good luck
5 Bronze
6 Xerxes
7 Peloponnesian
8 75

Page 37
Alexander's campaigns
a 2
b 8
c 1
d 3
e 5
f 4
g 6
h 7

Quick Quiz Answers

Once you have completed each page of quiz questions, check your answers below.

Page 38
History of Ancient Greece
1 d, b, a, c **2** b **3** d **4** b **5** b **6** c **7** e **8** a and c **9** c **10** c

Page 39
Cities and Rulers
1 d **2** c **3** c **4** a **5** d **6** b **7** c **8** b **9** d **10** c

Page 40
Greek Religion
1 b **2** c **3** d **4** c **5** c **6** d **7** b, d, e **8** b **9** a **10** c

Page 41
Daily Life
1 c **2** b **3** a **4** a and c **5** b **6** d **7** a **8** d **9** c **10** a **11** c

Page 42
Entertainment
1 d **2** c **3** d **4** b **5** c **6** a **7** b **8** a, b, e **9** a, d, e

Page 43
Greeks at Work
1 d **2** a **3** b **4** c **5** b **6** c **7** b **8** d **9** c **10** a and d

---

Acknowledgments

The publisher would like to thank the following:

Susan McKeever for assessing the manuscript, Monica Byles for proofreading, Philip Parker for 2020 consultant review, and Harish Aggarwal and Priyanka Sharma or the jacket.

The publisher would like to thank the following for their kind permission to reproduce their photographs:

(Key: a-above; b-below/bottom; c-center; l-left; r-right; t-top)

DK Images: British Museum 17br, 19br, 21bc, 21bl, 21c, 25cl, 28c, 28tr; Courtesy of The Science Museum 32cr; Rough Guides 1c, 6tr, 11ca, 21br, 32br; The Royal Ontario Museum, Toronto 1cl.

FAMOUS GREEKS

Name	Pythagoras	Socrates	Herodotus
Occupation	Mathematics	Philosophy	History
Famous for	Theory about right-angled triangles	Seeking wisdom and virtue by questioning beliefs	Father of history; wrote on the Persian wars
Dates	*c.* 580–490 BCE	*c.* 469–399 BCE	*c.* 484–425 BCE
Birthplace	Samos	Athens	Halicarnassus
Name	Aristotle	Plato	Thucydides
Occupation	Philosophy	Philosophy	History
Famous for	Founder of modern philosophy, tutor of Alexander the Great	Pupil of Socrates, founder of the Academy in Athens	History of Peloponnesian War between Athens and Sparta
Dates	384–322 BCE	*c.* 429–347 BCE	*c.* 460–395 BCE
Birthplace	Stagira	Athens	Athens
Name	Themistocles	Pericles	Solon
Ruled	Athens	Athens	Athens
Famous for	Creating the fleet that beat the Persians at Salamis	Masterminding Athens's rebuilding of the Acropolis	Laying the foundations of democracy in Athens
Dates	*c.* 524–459 BCE	*c.* 495–429 BCE	*c.* 640–558 BCE
Birthplace	Attica	Athens	Athens
Name	Leonidas	Peisistratos	Alexander the Great
Ruled	Sparta	Athens	Macedonia
Famous for	Heroic death at Thermopylae, outnumbered by the Persians	Popular tyrant who made Athens rich	Creating the Greek empire
Dates	*c.* 520–480 BCE	*c.* 607–527 BCE	356–323 BCE
Birthplace	Sparta	Athens	Pella

FAMOUS BUILDINGS

Name	Palace of Knossos	City of Mycenae	Parthenon Temple
Features	Labyrinth of the Minotaur	Home of Agamemnon; guarded by the Lion's Gate	Marble sculptures and statue of Athena by Phidias
Built by	Mythical architect Daedalus	According to legend, founded by Perseus	Architects Callicrates and Ictinos
Dates	c. 1900 BCE	c. 1800 BCE	c. 432 BCE
Location	Crete	Mainland Greece	Acropolis, Athens

Name	Theater at Epidaurus	Temple of Apollo	Sanctuary of Olympia
Features	Seated over 14,000 spectators	Delphic Oracle, where Apollo spoke through a priestess	Site of Olympic Games; statue of Zeus at Olympia
Built by	Polykleitos the younger	Architects Spintharos, Xenodoros, and Agathon	According to legend, King Pelops or Hercules or Zeus
Dates	4th century BCE	330 BCE	776 BCE
Location	Epidaurus	Delphi	Elis

FAMOUS ARTISTS

Name	Aeschylus	Aristophanes	Phidias
Occupation	Playwright	Playwright	Painting, sculpture, and architecture
Famous for	Founder of tragedy	Founder of comedy	Greatest of all classical sculptors
Dates	c. 525–456 BCE	c. 456–386 BCE	c. 480–430 BCE
Birthplace	Eleusis	Unknown, possibly Aegina	Unknown, probably Athens

Name	Sappho	Homer	Euripides
Occupation	Poetry	Epic poetry	Playwright
Famous for	Greatest female poet	Epic poems the Iliad and the Odyssey	Tragedies that were ahead of their time
Dates	c. 625–570 BCE	c. 8th century BCE	c. 480–406 BCE
Birthplace	Lesbos	Ionia, according to legend	Unknown, possibly Athens or Salamis